TEETHING PAINS

how to survive being a dad

Ben Wakeling

Published by Lulu.
ISBN 978-1-4475-3093-0

For Jessica, Isaac, Noah

and tired dads everywhere

CONTENTS

FOREWORD

You know those photos you sometimes see of meth addicts? The ones where you get the 'before' shot, when said addict isn't yet addicted and is all fresh-faced and relatively happy; and the 'after' shot, when their face looks like a walnut and their eyes point in different directions?

The very same photos could – pretty much - resemble you after one week of being a parent.

It's a sad fact of life that parenting is no easy task. In fact, after just one month of being a dad, your face is so drawn, lifeless and hollow that the only day of the year you fit in with everyone else is Halloween. However, it's an exciting time – and one which, honestly, you wouldn't change for the world.

Goodbye, Pert Breasts was my story of being an expectant dad; now, I've been thrust into the world of parenting. I hope my experiences match yours, and that together we can help each other through the quagmire that is being a dad in our child's early years, with only a few tears and only the hint of dark shadows under our eyes to show for it. That's the idea, anyway, but my genitals have been crushed by an over-excited toddler twice today, and it's only 9am.

Ben Wakeling

The ~~Rifleman's~~ Father's Creed

Prepare yourself for something truly genius.

Move aside, old man.

Those of you who are familiar with the American military or have ever seen *Full Metal Jacket* will be aware of the Rifleman's Creed. In a stroke of brilliance, I've adapted this to become the Father's Creed.

Well, kind of. All I've done is change the word 'rifle' for the word 'baby', but whatever. It's still awesome.

This creed must be recited every morning, ideally while you're holding your baby. Also, don't mumble: you need to shout this, preferably in a strong Texan accent. Don't worry about your mrs, or the neighbours. Just stand in front of the mirror, baby tucked under your arm, and bark at yourself like Sergeant Hartman.

So, without further ado, here is your creed. Pinky swear optional.

(I've missed out any bits about killing people; they seemed kinda unrelated and a bit scary.)

THE FATHERS CREED

This is my baby. There are many like it, but this one is mine.

My baby is my best friend. It is my life. I must master it as I must master my life. My baby, without me, is useless. Without my baby, I am useless. I must fire my baby true.

My baby is human, even as I, because it is my life. Thus, I will learn it as a brother. I will learn its weaknesses, its strength, its parts, its accessories, its sights and its barrel. I will ever guard it against the ravages of weather and damage as I will ever guard my legs, my arms, my eyes and my heart against damage. I will keep my baby clean and ready.

We will become part of each other.

SECTION ONE
BABY
(0-12 months)

This is a baby, although hopefully not yours.

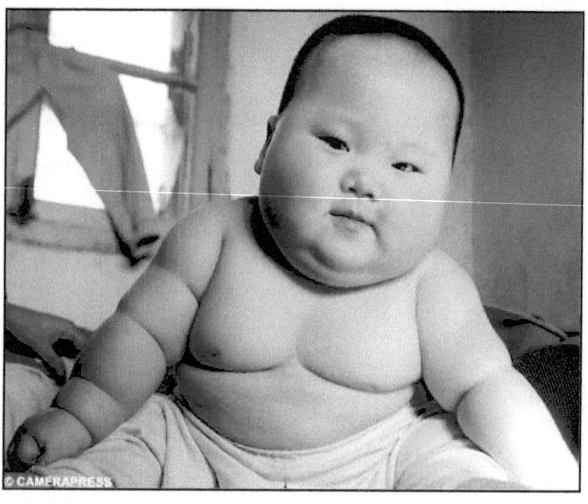

Sorry if it is actually yours. What on earth are you feeding it?

Before we start jabbering about babies, though, take a look in the mirror. Two nights of having a baby and you already look like the undead. You scare children when you walk past them. Cats arch their back when you approach. Sort yourself out.

Anyway, we're digressing already. So you're a dad, congratulations! Like every other dad around the world, you've realised pretty quickly that the 'bundle of joy' touted in the antenatal classes also comes with crying, pooping, burping, and throwing up; something that the midwives handily forgot to mention, something you could really do without, like that daft little bowl of salad they give you when you order a 12oz steak in your local restaurant.

Having a baby brings with it a million and one challenges, like Stephen Hawking being faced with a run of fifty hurdles. As well as spending most of your days and nights knuckle-deep in poo, you have to deal with the visitors, the added expenditure, and even a dose of male postnatal depression if you're *really* unlucky.

However, this is also a great opportunity to meet other dads, and bond with them over your mutual hatred of breast pumps, or swap stories about how your little guy or girl yakked all over your nice new suit. It's a time of unrivalled excitement as you watch your baby grow up, learning new things every day. It's a time when, suddenly, your priorities in life shift dramatically. It's a time when you unexplainably become super-sensitive whenever babies are mentioned, ruining your carefully honed masculine image. And it's a time of pity, as you find that your worst fears have been realised, and your precious one has inherited your nose.

Welcome to being a dad. Strap yourself in, keep your arms and legs inside the vehicle at all times, and smile for the camera. You're gonna love it.

BONDING WITH YOUR BABY

or, how to get your Jeong on

Phrases are often used casually nowadays. For example, people use the word 'hate' so freely that it's lost all meaning, and we now need to come up with a new word for how we feel when politicians start talking. Spotty and excitable teenagers talk of being 'Facebook raped', when friends log on as them and change their status to something embarrassing and unimaginative involving willies, maybe even change their profile photo to a naked old woman, or something. That kind of thing.

I'm sure she's beautiful on the inside.

"I'd kill for that" is another one, usually uttered by a breathless fat person on a treadmill who's eyeing up a pizza being chomped by someone in the distance. Of course they wouldn't *actually* kill for that, unless they were seriously desperate. (Although, on the other hand, you'd have to be pretty useless to be caught by an obese person. You'd hear them wheezing as they approached, for a start.)

When you have a baby, you realise the true meaning of "I'd kill for that". The mere thought of someone hurting your little boy or girl, even a tiny bit, leaves you frothing at the mouth like a rabid dog (or the fat person, incidentally). News stories about children being abused make your blood boil even more than they used to. If I ever think about someone hurting either of my two sons, my fists start to clench and I get a super-evil glare that could melt glass.

Say someone broke into your house and threatened your partner and baby. What would you do? Would you be worried about the law, or what could happen if you did everything in your power to stop any harm from coming to your family? I doubt it. You'd take 25 to life in a heartbeat if it meant your kid was OK.

This feeling of raw love and passion doesn't have a word in the English language, but the Koreans call it 'Jeong': the notion of loving someone so much you would give your life for them, even if they do drive you crazy.

But sometimes you don't feel that Jeong - that surge of love and emotion - straight away when your baby is born. Sometimes it comes days, weeks, even months after you become a dad, which can scare the living daylights out of you. You can feel like less of a man, like you've failed as a father in some way. The strange thing is, when it does come – and it will – it's instant, like someone flicking a switch.

I'll be honest with you: when my wife gave birth to Noah, it was a few days before I felt that father-son bond with him. I loved him, but there was no Jeong.

But it did come, and it wasn't during a momentous occasion such as him gripping my finger or smiling at me. One evening, my wife and I were in the living room when we heard Noah stirring and crying over the static of the baby monitor, and so I went upstairs to see to him.

As I approached the nursery door, the crying slowed to a few whimpers. I stopped in the doorway. He hadn't seen me, or sensed that I was there: he was just lying in his cot, clutching his muslin cloth and looking at the wall, blinking away a few tears, his breaths stuttering as he recovered from crying. And in that moment the switch was flicked. He seemed so fragile, so innocent, so utterly dependent on me. Here he was, suddenly alive and present in this big bad world, and he needed me to support him and give him strength. The bond was there, and I tiptoed to his bedside to gave him a lingering forehead kiss as my heart wrenched.

It's not uncommon for parents to not bond with their baby immediately, even mums – although they're probably just relieved to get it out, more than anything.

"I lost nine pounds in five minutes!"

Unfortunately, if you're struggling to bond with your baby, there's no step-by-step process that I can give you to magically result in you being overcome with joy. The only advice I can give is the same wisdom I impart to someone who's just had a nasty curry and is a bit concerned about the eventual repercussions: don't force it, it'll come in its own good time, and be prepared for it to burn a bit.

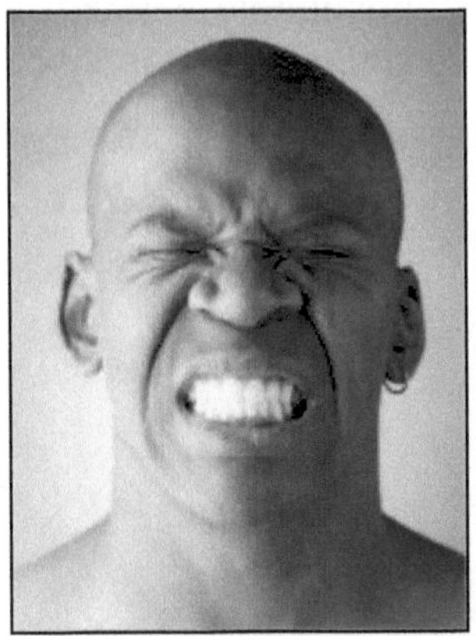

Although ignore the bit about burning. That's just curries.

All you can do is spend time with your child, some really good father-child contact. Talk to him (or her), feed him (assuming he's bottle fed, of course), play with him; whatever it takes, as you try to get your head around the fact that somehow you've put half of yourself into another person through the magic of reproduction.

MALE PND

It ain't no joke

My name is Ben, and I watch *Desperate Housewives*. Quite a big fan, in fact. I tell my wife that it has everything to do with the intricate storylines and absolutely nothing to do with the highly attractive and often scantily-clad women.

Wait...there are storylines?

However, between ogling Eva Longoria and fantasising about living in a house as big as those on Wisteria Lane, one sub-plot has arisen in one of the episodes somewhere that I've noticed. It concerns a father in the show, Tom Scavo, who - after the birth of his latest child - begins feeling a bit low. Eventually, he goes to the doctors to be diagnosed with what he thinks will be exhaustion. Instead, it turns out he has male postnatal depression.

I can almost hear mothers around the globe scoffing as they read that. "Postnatal depression?!" they exclaim, "But only mums get that! What will you men want next, periods?!"

I can confidently answer on behalf of all men when I say: no, thanks, we don't want periods.

Seriously. Keep your menstruation to yourself.

But male PND is real, so stop being mean!

What are the Symptoms of PND?

Admittedly, it's not as common in men as it is in women – with around 1 in 25 fathers demonstrating the symptoms of PND, compared to 1 in 10 for mothers; but the effects are no less detrimental to the health and mindset of the affected dad. The symptoms exhibited differ from person to person, but are largely identical to those shown by mothers: a sense of being overwhelmed and isolated, perhaps a lack of concentration (although that was probably something evident even *before* you had kids). Appetite is often affected, and time that is usually taken up with sleep is instead spent worrying.

The list of symptoms is comprehensive, and studies into male PND conclude that men are more likely to become hostile and aggressive in response to the symptoms they are experiencing as they struggle to come to terms with the radical life changes that they are going through. That's just how we react to things, as our tiny man brains can't understand what's going on.

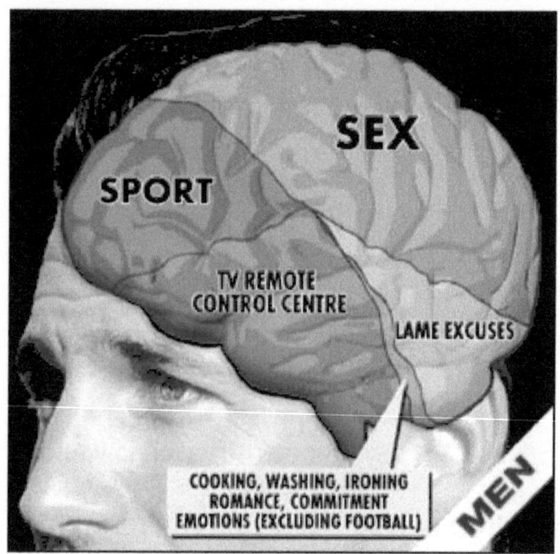

A man's brain, incidentally, looking a lot like this.

What are the effects of PND?

Postnatal depression can leave the father feeling useless and overwhelmed, and as a result there is a risk that he can become very introvert and withdrawn. This not only impacts the health of the father, but also has a negative effect on the development of his baby, who relies upon regular stimulation and interaction from both parents in order to boost cognitive function.

In 2008, a study entitled 'the Children of the 90s' by the University of Bristol found that postnatal depression in fathers can have long-lasting psychological effects on their children. Their findings have been released in two parts: the first, published in 2005, concluded that boys born to depressed fathers are twice as likely as their peers to develop behavioural problems by the age of three and a half.

The second half of this study elaborates on this, and suggests that these complications can continue into early adulthood. Paul Ramchandani, an Oxford University psychiatrist, is quoted in the results of the research as stating "conduct problems at this age are strongly predictive of later serious conduct problems, increased criminality and significantly increased societal costs."

Basically, if a dad has PND and it goes untreated, his kid could go on to be the next Al Capone.

How can PND be overcome?

There are a number of ways in which depression can be overcome – or, at the very least, managed to the extent that the effects are minimal. Health professionals encourage affected dads to not shy away from the problem, or assume that it is simply the result of a lack of sleep. They also, of course, warn against turning to drink or drugs as a way of alleviating the symptoms of PND; both mother and baby rely on the health of the father for development and support. Although we do enjoy a beer from time to time, so going *completely* tee-total would be a tad excessive.

Approaching a health professional is the best course of action, but takes courage, especially as some fathers feel that doing so would in some way compromise their masculinity. However, it is the best thing to do, and fathers suffering from PND will find relief and support in being able to share their stories with others going through a similar situation.

So don't be mean to us if we seem a bit down following the birth of a child, or refer to us as a "big girl's blouse". Instead, tell us to put down the Jack Daniels and see a doctor. It could be the difference between your kids growing up to be *Same Difference* or Bonnie and Clyde.

Although the jury's still out on which are worse.

FEMALE PND

Also not a joke

I have been lucky enough not to know what postnatal depression is like first-hand, although I gather it ain't much of a picnic.

As I mentioned in the last chapter, there's about a ten percent chance that your mrs will get postnatal depression, usually developing within the first month after childbirth. The 'baby blues' is one thing, demonstrated in around half of new mothers. It lasts for a few hours, a few days at the most; roughly the same amount of time it takes to get over the fact that England have crashed out of yet another World Cup.

It's coming home...maybe, one day.
Probably not in our lifetime.
If ever.

But postnatal depression is something completely different, and much more severe. If your partner develops it, it could have a lasting and detrimental impact on your relationship as a couple and a family, so it's important to be as supportive as possible if this occurs.

What are the symptoms?

Why, thanks for asking, I'll tell you. A lot of these symptoms are just generally exhibited by females anyway, so you may have a little struggle identifying PND; but you'll figure it out eventually, once you've stopped leaving your rubbish lying around and the toilet seat up, you pig.

- Mums with PND feel low or miserable for no apparent reason, sometimes becoming tearful. This may be more obvious in the morning.
- Irritability is also a telling symptom of PND, but then again, this is almost constant in all ladies around the globe. *(Avoids withering glare)*
- Mums with PND may find it difficult to go to sleep even when they are tired, or wake up really early.
- PND sufferers often feel lethargic and weak.
- Mothers with PND often feel anxious and tense all the time, maybe even suffering panic attacks.
- A feeling of being unable to cope, without any light at the end of the tunnel.

The good thing is PND is treatable; but the mum will need help to get through it...and this is where you come in.

How can I help if my mrs has PND?

Alright, now you're just interrupting.

There are many ways in which you can give your partner a helping hand if she is struggling with parenthood and suffering from PND. First and foremost, don't make a sad face by pulling down the corners of your mouth whenever you see her. That will *not* go down well.

Let's crack on with the bullet points, as our tiny pea-brained male minds can only absorb little pieces of information:

- Get as much info as you can about PND, so you know what she is going through and the treatments available.
- Encourage her to speak to a professional (such as her GP or health visitor) about how she's feeling, and go with her to any appointments if she wants you to.
- Give her a hand with night feeding by giving your child expressed breast milk or formula milk, so your mrs can get some sleep.
- Help around the house with day-to-day chores, but be careful not to take over.
- Make sure she's eating healthily and getting three main meals a day down her.
- Give her a back massage, or even just a cuddle.
- Provide constant reassurance, a listening ear, and patience.
- Take the baby out for the day so she can spend some time relaxing.
- Recognise that there'll be good and bad days, so take the rough with the smooth.

Don't abandon your own needs when helping your partner though PND, though. Ask a friend or member of the family to take your baby/kids for a few hours each week to give you and your mrs time alone as a couple. As well as this, take some time out for yourself to help gather your thoughts and stay positive. Also, to drink beer.

INTRODUCING YOUR KID TO YOUR NEW BABY

I am, of course, talking about this kind of kid:

Not this kind of kid.

In case there was any confusion – although there are similarities, if you look closely.

We were always a bit concerned about how our eldest son, Isaac – coming up to 3 at the time – would react upon meeting Noah for the first time. Would they get along? Would Isaac get jealous of the attention that we would have to give Noah? Would he not care at all?

It was with some trepidation, then, that I held Noah as Isaac came into the living room to meet his brother for the first time. Isaac wandered in, and spotted 'Baby Noah'. We'd told him what had happened, so it wasn't a total shock. He ran over, looked him up and down, laughed, and then went off to play with his toys. A little later on, he came back to give him a hold. And they've been inseparable ever since.

Sorry about Isaac's 'camera smile'.

Our fears are shared with every parent who has ever had to introduce their young child to a newborn and were unsure what the reaction would be; which is why it is important to gradually prepare your child for the new arrival instead of surprising them. Here's what you can do to keep the eye-scratching to a minimum.

Before Your Baby is Born

It is important that you and your mrs begin to plant the seed of a new little brother or sister in the brain of your child as soon as possible, to give them time to mull it over and get their heads around it. Also, it'll go some way to explaining to the poor kid why mummy cries all the time at nothing while her tummy gradually expands.

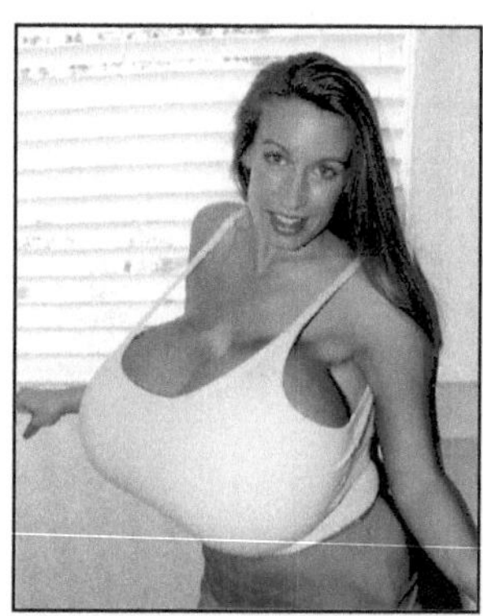

But not why her lovebags are so gigantic.

Don't expect a massive reaction when you tell your child there's a baby on the way, though. Kids get excited about sweets, fish and wrapping paper, as opposed to if mum's up the duff or not; so don't be put out if your kid looks at you blankly instead of fist-pumping the air and yelling "YESSS!!" once you've broken the news.

As an illustration of this point, I imagine the conversation with my mum when I was told about the imminent arrival of my younger sister went something like this (I was 5 at the time):

Mum: "Ben, come here. I've got something to tell you."

I shuffle over, looking really really cute.

Me: "What is it, mummy?" *(still cute)*

Mum: "I'm going to have a baby! You're going to have a little brother or sister!"

I pause, and press my fingertips together in some kind of Alan Sugar power stance.

Me: "OK…will I still get fed?"

Mum: *(bemused)* "Why…yes, of course."

Me: "S'alright then. Nice work on getting knocked up. That explains those weird sounds I heard."

Exit stage right.

Y'welcome.

The thing is, kids aren't really bothered about stuff that doesn't directly affect them, and so to make the first meeting extra special you need to find some things for your child to get excited about, such as:

- It's someone new to play with when younger and torment when older;
- They'll have someone to look after, and therefore be a big grown up boy/girl;

- They will be a big brother or sister, which is just the most super-awesomest thing in the world EVER. (You get my drift.)

We also encouraged Isaac to say goodnight to Noah while Jess was pregnant, and even sing to him from time to time, which was super-sweet when he did it, but not-so-sweet when I laid down a bit of Jay-Z in my velvety 'from the hood' tones.

Another good way to let your child know what's about to happen is to read some books to them on the subject. In a nice voice, though. If you do it in a scary voice, you won't be reassuring at all.

Also try not to be overly aggressive.

After Your Baby is Born

Some mums feel that the best way to introduce their child to the newborn is to have them present in the room during childbirth. My mother did not decide on this course of action for me, for which I will be forever grateful.

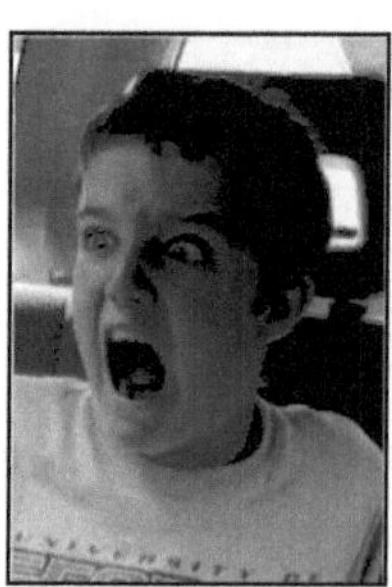

Otherwise I'd have looked a bit like this.

Most parents, though, will be introducing child to newborn after the screaming is over and the various fluids have been mopped up. Here are some handy tips on making sure it doesn't all go pear-shaped.

- If you have a young child, encourage them to draw a picture as a gift to their new brother or sister.
- Buy a gift from the new baby to the older sibling (I still remember getting a Tonka Truck when my sister was born - it was freaking awesome).
- Have someone else hold the baby when your child first enters – they are more likely to kick off if they see you holding and cooing over a new child and not them. Also, by 'someone else' I mean someone related or familiar, not any old stranger.
- Tell your child that you've 'brought someone to see them' – this will make it seem as if the baby is excited to see their sibling (when in reality it can barely see past its own little button nose).
- Let your child hold the new baby as soon as you can and have as much contact with it as possible. Your child is more likely to form a bond if they can touch and feel the new arrival, as well as cementing the fact that the baby is real.
- Include your older child with activities involving your newborn, such as washing or nappy changing. This will help make them feel appreciated.
- Spend time with your older child, just the two of you. Leave the newborn with your partner and devote a couple of hours or so to your child, so they don't feel left out.

These hints will help everything go swimmingly when you introduce your kids for the first time, as well as boosting the formation of a friendship between the two. I can't guarantee that there won't be any awkward silences; not least when your child looks at you and says something along the lines of "Daddy, how are babies made?"

"Y'see, son, it's like...umm...you've got this stork, right?"

BABY NECESSITIES

Number One: a baby

There are certain things that would be handy to have back at your house for when your baby comes home, otherwise you'll be carrying him or her around in a Tesco bag, which isn't a good look (you could at least go with a Bag for Life, you cheapskate).

Now, look: I know that the only *real* necessities are love and a caring family. I've been told off for not mentioning this in the past, mostly by long-haired mothers called Rain, or Stream, or something equally as hippy. But the fact of the matter is, unless you're a caveman or a member of a remote Amazonian tribe, you'll need a few more things to help the early weeks go smoothly. So here they are.

But first, a list of necessities for **you**! Man, I keep you lot on your toes.

Things for You/the Mrs...

...because you've got to look after yourself as well, otherwise your kid will grow up thinking he has Lurch for a father.

The first thing you should get ready is a **few extra meals**. You can either make and freeze them before the due date so you just have to lob them in the oven, or stock up on some of those oh-so-healthy microwave meals that taste of salt and little else. As you are fully aware by now, a baby sucks up any ounce of spare time you ever had before, which can often result in your evening meal being whatever you can find ground into the carpet or down the back of the sofa.

Babies are little, and prone to illness and infection. It's therefore a good idea to have a few of those little bottles of **sanitising gel** around the house, so you can clean your hands every now and then after you've picked your nose or scratched your bum. It also means you can pretend, if but for a moment, to be a surgeon.

Unless you actually *are* a surgeon, in which case you've got far more money than I have.

Get yourself some **sanitary pads**. Not for you, of course, unless you're menstruating, in which case you should probably pay a visit to that surgeon shown in the rather amusing photo above. Your mrs might continue to bleed after she's given birth – known as 'lochia' – and this can go on for 4 to 6 weeks; and so, passing over a pad and winking will turn you into some kind of superhero in her eyes. Tampons should not be used, though, as they can cause infection. Instead, stick them up your nose and have a jolly good laugh.

Also stock up on **nipple pads**. Again, not for you, you weirdo. You'll be able to tell by those gradually increasing wet patches over your partner's boobs that she's leaking. Get a pad on 'em.

Things For Your Baby

Because you can't carry it around in a bag, yeah, yeah, we've already discussed this.

A **car seat** is essential, as strapping your baby to a roof rack to bring it home from the hospital or take it out and about is almost definitely against the law.

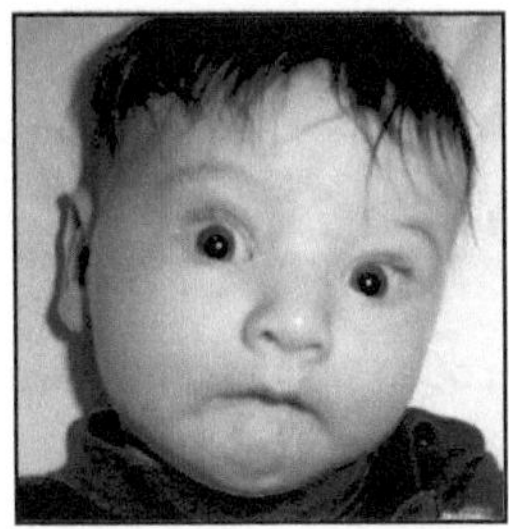

But will result in a face like this.

Make sure it meets all the latest laws and regulations, though, and work out how to fit it before your baby arrives, or you'll get yourself mega stressed.

Buy a **cot** so your little 'un has somewhere to sleep, preferably one with a side that raises and lowers so you don't have to break your back just to lift him out. Be warned: Americans call the cot a 'crib'. I don't really know why. Crazy Americans.

A cot itself is pretty useless without a **mattress** and **waterproof cover** for your baby to actually lie on – otherwise it might fall through the slats, which would be pretty bad. Any accidents that happen will not soak the mattress due to the cover, so cleaning up won't be too much of a problem.

Bedding and blankets are also a good shout. Not much else I can say about them.

Layette is a fancy word that basically means baby clothing. Your baby will grow pretty quickly in the first few weeks of its life, so buy some onesies a few sizes bigger so he can grow into them. Also stock up on socks, hats, and mittens (if your baby scratches his face a lot).

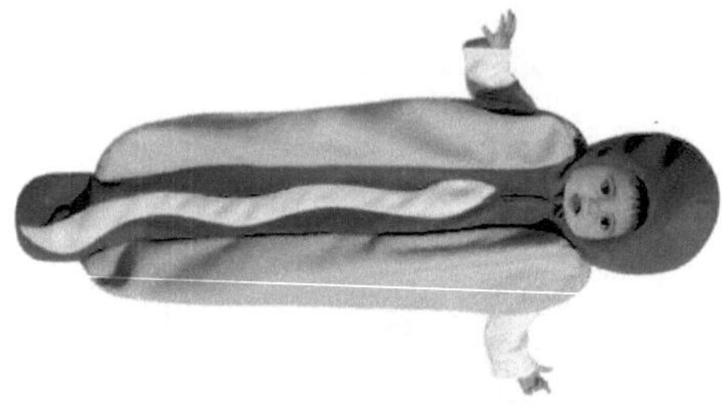

Hotdog outfit optional, but awesome.

Estimates reckon that a new baby will go through about 70 **nappies** a week for the first six weeks, and 50 a week thereafter, so you'll need to get a few bags bought. Be warned: nappy manufacturers know that you're not going to let your baby poo on the floor, so they price their nappies pretty darn high. Scoundrels.

Baby wipes and **nappy rash cream** will give you a means to actually wipe revolting turds off your baby's buttocks, and a method for soothing the accompanying stinging (we've all been there). You might want to clean your baby's bits with **cotton wool balls** dipped in water for the first few weeks.

Buying a **pram** or **baby carrier** is a good idea for getting your kid out and about while keeping your hands free (apart from the pram thing).

If you're bottle feeding, buy some **formula** in advance, as well as the **bottles** and **teats** (snigger). Again, expensive. This will be a running theme throughout your child's life.

Chances are your baby will pick up a bug at some point, and so buying a **thermometer** is a good shout, along with any other **medical supplies** you reckon you might need. There's a chapter somewhere in this book that explains in more detail how to know if your baby is ill.

Finally, get yourself and your mrs a **changing bag** so you can whip out a nappy and all the associated items when your baby poos on the bus.

That's everything...I think. All this stuff should last you about a week. Because life's just that fair.

Still awesome.

DEALING WITH VISITORS

How to be polite while being rude in your head

You know how, when you get chucked out of a nightclub, the bouncer will grab you by your collar and literally throw you onto the street, followed by your coat and shoes? There will be times while visitors are in your house that you will feel like doing the same. A word of advice: don't. Your Great Aunt Mabel has a dodgy hip and would not appreciate being lobbed out of your front door and getting a mouthful of tarmac. Also, she's 86. Leave her alone.

86, and crazy.

The thing is, babies are people magnets; and pretty much as soon as you're home you'll have friends and family scratching at your door trying to get in to see your kid. While this can be nice, the first few days after birth are a crucial time for bonding with your baby and settling into family life. Excessive numbers of visitors can disrupt this, as well as being super-annoying.

So what to do? Set up a complex laser system to zap any approaching visitors? Watch at the window, then as they walk towards the door open your letterbox and yell "NOOOOO!!"? Pretend you don't know who they are when you open the door? For example:

> "Sorry, who are you?"
> "I'm your mother, you idiot!"
> "Hmm, no you're not. My mother is beautiful and sexy. You're leathery and old."

Et cetera. The list is endless.

The problem is twofold: once you let a visitor in, they'll stay for hours. Secondly, they'll have their gross germy hands all over you new baby's nice soft skin. But fear not: all this can be overcome with a bit of careful planning, and the odd firm word. This is how you deal with the dreaded visitor plague.

Cut Off All Communication

This is where, basically, you and your family shut yourselves off from the outside world for a week or two while you have time to gel and bond as a family. You could even give it a cool name, like Operation Blackout, if you like. Even answering the phone is out of bounds: instead, you record a short voicemail message that gives the name and weight of the baby, and lets the caller know you're all well.

Whilst a good idea in theory, this option would be pretty difficult to put into practice. As well as seeming a bit weird, you'll all get cabin fever being stuck in the house all by yourselves, and without regular exposure to daylight your skin will go all grey and lifeless, like some kind of parental zombie.

Set Visiting Hours

Visiting hours aren't limited to hospitals, you know. A great way of at least regulating how long the guests stay at your place is to enforce strict visiting hours. This gives you all time to relax and settle in to family life, as well as giving you the opportunity to look respectable for when visitors do arrive.

Alternatively, you could always stick a note on your front door simply saying that mum and baby are asleep, so back off (or 'do not disturb', if you want to be all traditional and polite about it). You'd be surprised how many visitors back off when reading it, especially if you use terribly offensive language.

"WHY would he SAY THAT?!"

Drag Yourself into the 21st Century

I heard a rumour recently that there are these things called social network sites, where you can swap stories and photos and whimsical messages. There's one called Face Book, another about tweeting and there's even the You Tube.

Ain't I funny. But these sites can be valuable when staving off the inevitable influx of visitors. 'Look, but don't touch' is my motto, which I strictly live by, which is why it's such a wonder that Jess ever got pregnant in the first place.

If you're happy with having a photo of your baby on the Internet, then get it on there. At the very least, it'll keep people contented until they get past the looking stage and want to physically poke your baby in the face. You can also use Skype to make a video call to relatives, who will be blissfully unaware that you're naked from the waist down.

But, unavoidably, some visitors *will* breach your threshold and manage to barge their way into your house. So here's what you can do to make them get out again.

Wash Your Hands

OK, so this bit isn't about getting them to leave, but is important nonetheless. As I mentioned before, no matter how sanitary these visitors think they are their hands are going to be humming with germs, so it's a good idea to insist that they use an antiseptic gel to clean their fingers before they go spreading them all over your newborn.

Make Up An Appointment

Visitors will come, and they will invariably outstay their welcome – which, to be fair, only lasted about 30 seconds anyway, so they didn't ever stand much of a chance.

If you really want to get rid of someone, make sure you mention to them as soon as they come in that they can only stay for, say, half an hour, as your mrs has an appointment to get to. You don't even have to say what the appointment is for, if you don't feel like making something up. Which could be fun.

Put Baby Down

No, not in the veterinarian way! Gosh. I mean for a nap.

Let's face it: the visitors aren't here to see you, or your mrs. In fact, by this point, you both probably look so knackered and dishevelled they may well avoid eye contact with you altogether. So if you put your baby down for a nap, it won't be long before whoever has come round will lose interest and leave. Ta-dah! Your house is empty. Apart from you, of course. And the mrs. And your bab - oh, you know what I mean.

Insist They Bring Food

'Cos everything's better when you're eating a burger.

As demonstrated by this enthusiastic gentleman.

HEALTH VISITS

Or, Why that woman's poking my baby

One of the great things about the NHS is the aftercare that your wife and baby get once you're out of hospital. I imagine in other countries, like icy Eastern European nations with unpronounceable names, you get shoved out of the hospital doors and left to fend for yourself before you've even had a chance to clean the goo off your baby's head.

Even the bears aren't safe.
(Every caption I write makes less sense.)

I apologise, of course, if you're Eastern European and I've just offended you. But my point is that professional care for both mum and baby doesn't stop once you're all at home – at least not in the UK. Every mum will receive a number of home visits and postnatal checks to make sure that she's healing up nicely and that baby's growing as well as it should. The frequency of visits tends to differ from region to region, so have a chat with your midwife if you're unsure of how many you'll get.

But let's start from the very beginning. Your baby is but a minute old, and already the checks have started.

The Apgar Checks

These checks will probably be carried out without you even noticing. At one minute and five minutes after birth, the midwife will assess your baby, looking at various things such as skin colour, heart rate, and muscle tone.

Each category is scored between 0 and 2, and then the scores are totted up at the end. It's a way of quickly assessing whether or not your baby needs any additional treatment.

Here's the Apgar scale. You'll notice that the first letter of each indication spells the word 'APGAR'. I'm almost certain this is simply a coincidence.

Indication	Score of 0	Score of 1	Score of 2
Skin colour			
Appearance	Blue all over	White at extremities, body pink	Pink all over
Heart rate			
Pulse	Absent	Slow	Fast
Reflex response			
Grimace	No response to stimulation	Grimacing when stimulated	Crying and coughing
Muscle tone			
Activity	Limp	Some bending or stretching of limbs	Active movement
Breathing			
Respiration	Absent	Weak or irregular	Good, baby is crying

Any score from 7-10 is very good, although you'll be after the perfect 10, I'm sure. Scores between 5-7 may result in the baby being given oxygen or just vigorously rubbed by the midwife, which actually sounds quite nice.

Any babies who score a 5 or below will need additional help and care, and placed on a mat in a specialised trolley. This will provide heat, light and oxygen to help your baby along.

The Heel Prick Test

As if having been squeezed through a slimy birth canal isn't enough, a day or so after he is born your baby will have to endure the heel prick test.

A tiny amount of blood is taken from your baby's heel (go figure), and tested for a number of things:

- Phenylketonuria, an enzyme deficiency;
- A thyroid deficiency;
- Sickle cell disorders;
- Cystic fibrosis, which affects the lungs and digestive system;
- Medium Chain Acyl Dehydrogenase Deficiency – or MCADD for short, which is a rare condition (around 1 in 10,000) that affects the way the body converts fat into energy.

My eldest son slept through his heel prick test; Noah screamed the place down. I was quite calm on both occasions, but didn't get a sticker or anything.

The Newborn Examination

Between 4 and 48 hours following your baby's birth a midwife or paediatrician will check your kid from head to toe to make sure all is well. Here's the rundown of what they'll check:

Head

The midwife will check the shape of your baby's head. A head that looks slightly squashed is very common in newborns – your head would look a little funky too if you'd just rammed it through the equivalent of a drainpipe. A head that is squashed or 'moulded' will right itself in around 48 hours.

The fonatelles (soft spot) will also be checked. Any bruises on your baby's head caused by the ventouse or forceps will clear up in their own time.

Ears and Eyes

First check: make sure there's two of each.

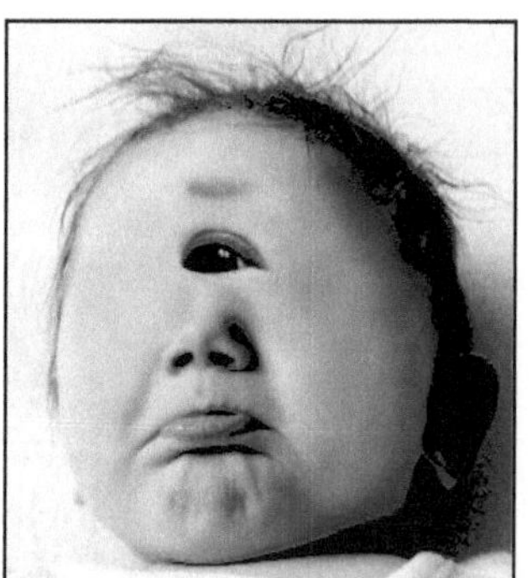

"Doctor's note: Baby seems to have ruffled hair. Also, one eye. Concerned about the hair."

The midwife/doctor will use an ophthalmoscope (that pointy instrument with the light) to shine a light into your baby's eyes to check for 'red reflex' – the same kind of 'red eye' effect you see if you take a photo at the wrong angle. The presence of the red eye means that any eyesight illnesses, such as cataracts, are not present. A good thing, of course.

Many midwives and doctors will give your baby a hearing test before your mrs is discharged, but if this doesn't happen, one will be given by the health visitor.

Mouth

The doctor will check whether your baby's palate (roof of mouth) is completely formed, and the only way to do this is to get her index finger right in there and have a good old rummage, which looks a tad weird. She's checking for any gaps, which could indicate a cleft palate, a condition which will need surgery to correct.

The doctor will also check your baby's tongue for a condition known as tongue-tie (or 'ankyloglossia', if you want to be posh about it), where the piece of skin that anchors your tongue to the bottom of your mouth is further forward than normal, limiting tongue mobility.

Heart and Lungs

Next, your baby's heart is checked to make sure it's beating rhythmically and that there are no sounds or murmurs that shouldn't be there. A stethoscope is also used to make sure that air is entering both lungs clearly and equally.

Heart murmurs are quite common as your baby's circulatory system adapts to birth. In the womb, both sides of the heart beat together; but they begin to function separately once your baby is born. Because of this, your baby's heart is working pretty hard, and so the odd murmur may exist. They should settle down and disappear without any outside help, but your doctor might schedule a follow-up examination just to be on the safe side.

Genitals

This check isn't to establish whether your baby has genitals. Hopefully, you and your mrs have already made this check before deciding upon which name to go for. And unless your child has a crotch as smooth as Action Man, it'll be either a boy or a girl.

This photo has very little to do with this section, but remains due to awesomeness.

It's common for your baby's bits to be swollen or dark after birth. Some babies even have temporary boobs, believe it or not, which conjures up some very bizarre images in one's mind.

Your health visitor or midwife will check for undescended testes in boys, and will check his willy to make sure the hole's on the end and not underneath – which would give you the ability to pee round corners, but wouldn't go down great with the ladies.

Whoever carries out the test will check your baby's anus to make sure it's formed correctly, and ask you if he or she (the baby, that is) has urinated or passed any poo since birth.

I am so glad we've got that section out of the way. It was getting weird.

Skin

Your baby's skin will be checked to see if he or she has any birthmarks, including V-shaped marks on the back of the neck (known as stork marks) and any Mongolian spots (dark patches on the buttocks, common amongst East Africans, East Asians and Polynesians, hence the whole Mongolia thing).

Hands and Feet

Invariably, one of the first things you do as a parent is to count the fingers and toes to make sure there's ten of each.

Yes, I know technically it's eight fingers and two thumbs, but get a life.

The examiner will also check for webbing between the fingers and toes, as well as making sure that there are two creases on each of his palms. One palmar crease could be an indication of Down's syndrome - but there would also be other physical signs to back this up.

The doctor will examine the position of your baby's feet and ankles when he is resting. A foot that is turned in and down could present a case of club foot, which can be treated relatively easily - although may take some time.

Spine and Hips

Your baby's spine will be checked to make sure it is nice and straight. It is common for newborns to have a small indentation at the base of the spine; this is known as a sacral dimple, and is harmless as well as common. If the dimple is quite deep, however, your baby may be sent for further checks as there could be a problem with the development of the spinal cord.

The examiner will then waggle your baby's legs around in an attempt to assess whether his hips are stable and flexible. I like to think that wee baby Elvis simply stood up and gyrated in order to demonstrate his pelvic health.

Thank you very muuuuch.

Reflexes

This is the part where your baby is dropped from a short height to see if it lands on all fours. I jest! That's just for kittens.

Whilst your baby is born with a number of natural reflexes – sucking and grasping, for example – the examiner will most likely carry out what's known as the Moro reflex. This is where she allows your baby's head to fall backwards a short distance – obviously catching him, of course.

Your baby should respond by holding out both arms and spreading his fingers, as well as stretching out his legs. I remember seeing the health visitor carry out this test on Noah. I was all like, "tut...butterfingers". Then I worked out what she was doing.

Your First Postnatal Health Visit

You may find that your doula (if you have one) visits every day for a short while after your baby is born, but the first NHS-style visit will be when your little guy or girl is about 10-15 days old.

The health visitor will closely examine your baby, essentially making sure that it's all in one piece and is healthy. The tests carried out will be the same as those detailed in the last section, and is simply to make sure your newborn is progressing well.

It's a good idea to have your Personal Child Health Record book handy (the red one) as the health visitor will need to note down a few records so that your baby's progress can be tracked over time.

Your mrs may be asked how well feeding is going, and how you're all getting along as a family. Resist the urge to burst into tears; it doesn't look good.

The Six-Week Checkup

This checkup is designed to make sure that mum and baby are both healthy, and that your partner has healed well.

For blokes, this is the point where your mrs could be given the green light to get jiggy with you again. But seriously, don't expect this to happen. Not for a while, at least. I've devoted a whole chapter to this issue somewhere in this book, as it gets many dads incredibly frustrated, and many women feeling like they've got a horny pet lingering around the house. No, I'm not going to tell you where it is! Find it yourself! Man, you're lazy.

The Nine-Month Checkup

Guess when this checkup takes place.

This checkup is much like the others, in that the health visitor will be weighing and measuring your baby, checking his eyesight and hearing, and answering any queries you have. Expect questions on how well he's sleeping, eating, whether he's crawling, what he says, and so on. There's no right or wrong answer; the health visitor is merely there to assess your baby's development and dish out some advice – so don't freak out if your little man or lady isn't crawling yet.

So those are your basic health visits – for the first year, anyway. You may get more, if your baby needs a closer eye on him, but this is a rare occurrence. So now you know why that woman's poking her finger in your child's mouth, why she's so interested in whether or not his testes are swollen, and why she couldn't give a monkeys about yours.

BABY VACCINATIONS

Polio is a great baby name

Unfortunately, for the first few years of your baby's life, he or she will have had more needles poked into him than Amy Winehouse on a night out. However, unlike national treasure Amy, the substances being injected into your baby's bloodstream are incredibly beneficial, and will protect against potentially fatal diseases.

But which vaccinations does your baby have? When does he have them? And what the heck is Diptheria anyway?

Alright, alright, pipe down. First off, let's give you a schedule of the free vaccinations currently on offer in the UK, and when.

2 Months

- Diptheria, tetanus, pertussis (also known as whooping cough), polio and Haemophilus influenza type B. Given as a single jab known in medical circles as DTaP/IPV/Hib
- Pneumococcal infection

3 Months

- Second dose of DTaP/IPV/Hib
- Meningitis C

4 Months

- Third dose of DTaP/IPV/Hib
- Second dose against Pneumococcal infection
- Second dose against Meningitis C

12-13 Months

- Third dose against Meningitis C
- Fourth dose against Haemophilus influenza type B (this and the Meningitis C dose are given in the same jab)
- Measles, mumps and rubella (MMR), single jab
- Third dose against Pneumococcal infection

3 Years, 4 Months

- Second dose against MMR
- Diptheria, tetanus, pertussis and polio, a 4-in-1 jab

Which illnesses are being prevented?

It's all very well knowing the names of the diseases and conditions being prevented against, but the importance of these vaccinations hits home when you discover just what these nasty bugs can do if they get into your baby's system.

Diptheria

Diptheria is a contagious bacterial infection, beginning with a sore throat before leading on to respiratory issues and difficulty swallowing. It could cause damage to the heart and nervous systems.

Haemophilus Influenzae type B

Despite the rather sweet nickname 'Hib', this infections can cause a number of illnesses, one of the worst being bacterial meningitis. Before the vaccine was introduced, Hib was the main cause of meningitis in kids under two years old.

Measles

You are probably familiar with measles: symptoms include a rash and a fever, much like chickenpox. What you perhaps don't know is that it can kill, and one in 15 children with measles can go on to have complications such as fits, chest infections and brain damage.

Meningitis C

Or Meningococcal C conjugate, to give you its full name. It's a type of bacteria that can cause nasty illnesses such as meningitis (obviously) and septicaemia. This vaccination does not protect against meningitis caused by a viral infection or other strains of bacteria.

Mumps

I had mumps once, and spent a good few days looking like Professor Klump.

Just without the sweet smile.

Mumps, as with many illnesses, is no fun, and is characterised by fever, headache, vomiting and swollen glands in the face and neck. The swelling usually goes after a few days, but there is a danger that it could spread to other parts of the body – including the brain.

Pertussis

Better known as 'whooping cough', this is an acute respiratory infection characterised by – yes, you guessed it – a pretty severe cough. This can cause choking, vomiting and difficulty with breathing.

Pneumococcal Infection

This disease is spread via coughing or sneezing, and can lead to pneumococcal meningitis, septicaemia and pneumonia. All the more reason to vaccinate against the little blighter.

Polio

Nothing to do with pressed mints with a hole cut out, a popular Volkswagen model, or riding around like a ponce on the back of a horse.

You're thinking of Polo.

Polio attacks the nervous system, and is common in developing countries with poor sanitation, as it is transmitted from person to person via human poo. Thankfully, polio has been eradicated in the UK.

Rubella

Also known as 'German measles', rubella has the symptoms of a swollen neck and pink rash. While it's unlikely to cause your child immediate harm, you should make sure that your children are protected: if a pregnant woman contracts rubella her unborn child could be harmed.

Tetanus

Tetanus enters the body through cuts or burns on the skin, as it is caused by bacterial spores often found in soil. It causes painful muscular contractions and spasms, beginning in the jaw and neck (which is why it is also known as 'lockjaw'), and continuing to the chest, back and lower body.

What are the Side Effects?

The risk of side effects with these vaccinations is very low, with allergic responses equally as rare.

Many injections simply leave an area that may become red and swollen, which will last for a few days. Some babies get a mild fever for up to ten days after the injections. Headaches are also common, as well as symptoms that resemble a cold; some may react particularly badly to jabs by suffering from loss of appetite or a rash.

Vaccination protects your kids for a long, long time against some of the world's nastiest illnesses. Of course, it is your right to refuse vaccinations, but - as I always say - if it's free, take it. Unless the free thing is being handed out by a dodgy-looking guy leading me into an empty van.

Although I may have a think about it first.

HOW TO KNOW IF YOUR BABY IS ILL

Hint: It pukes. A lot.

Babies, like women, cry a lot.

Especially after watching *Toy Story 3*.

As a parent, you become attuned to the different cries that your baby has: you can tell if he has trapped wind, is hungry, or is just crying for the hell of it, because – let's face it – they can't do much else.

Sometimes, though, the crying will be an indication that your baby is feeling a bit under the weather; but, unless your baby is super-advanced, he can't tell you where it hurts. That would be pretty cool, though, if he could speak. You'd be like "Hey, what's the matter?" and your baby would go "Yeah, it's my gut, it's playing up, and I feel a little nauseous. Also, I've pood myself."

Until these cyborg-super-babies exist, we dads are going to have to rely on some simple indications that something isn't quite right. These are listed below, because I'm helpful like that.

Temperature

While midwives and health professionals may tell you to touch your baby's chest to figure out if he has a temperature, the most accurate and fool-proof way is, of course, to use a thermometer.

Just to make life that little more awkward, there are a number of different types of thermometer on the market for you to choose from, each of which are more or less accurate and expensive than the other.

Scan strip thermometers are widely used, and placed on baby's forehead. A number corresponding to his or her temperature is then illuminated by some kind of strange magical force. While these are great for day-to-day readings, they're not completely accurate – they measure the temperature of the skin, not of the body.

Aural thermometers (i.e. you stick them in your baby's ear) are, on the other hand, very accurate – but also pretty expensive, and will set you back the best part of £40-£50.

Your best bet is a digital thermometer. It's only a tenner for a decent one, and you can get an accurate reading by placing it under your baby's armpit or in their mouth, if they're still enough.

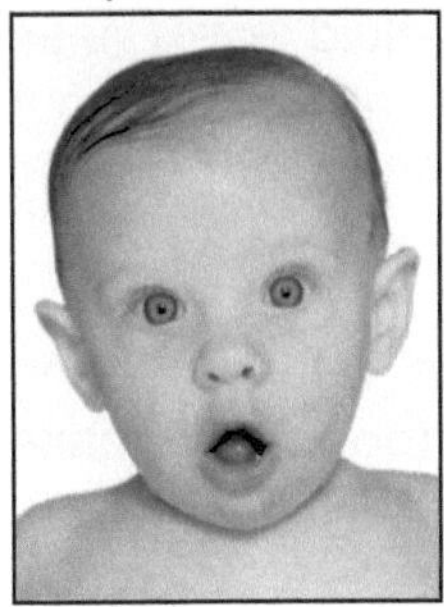

Research has shown, though, that the most accurate reading can be obtained by sticking the tip of the thermometer up your baby's backside: but good luck with that. Also, you're bound to forget and pop the thermometer in your mouth next time you're feeling a bit peaky.

What classes as a high temperature?

Your baby's normal temperature should be between 36 and 37ºC (96.8 – 98.6ºF), depending on where on their body you are taking it, and you might find that it goes up or down by a degree during the day. In fact, in some cases, a higher body temperature can increase the baby's production of germ-fighting cells, thus reducing the length of an illness.

A temperature over 37.5ºC (99.5ºF) is classed as a fever, and you should get in touch with your GP or health visitor if his or her temperature reaches 38ºC (101ºF) or higher if they're under three months, and 39ºC (102ºF) if they're three to six months old.

What other indications are there?

If you do not have a thermometer to hand, you can identify if your baby has a fever if they display the following symptoms:

- A flushed appearance
- Irritability/crying
- Clammy skin/sweating
- Tiredness

What can I do to bring down a fever?

The main thing to do when your baby has a fever is to encourage it to drink as much as possible - even if it is just little and often – as their fluid levels need to be kept at a normal level. Keep an eye on your baby's nappies – if they're dry, she's not getting enough fluids.

Paracetomol or ibuprofen can be used to bring down a fever and relieve pain, but (obviously) make sure you give the correct dosage.

As well as this, you can also do these things to bring down a nasty high temperature:

- Undress them to their nappy.
- Cover them with a sheet, if necessary.
- Keep the room well aired, and at a temperature of around 18°C (65°F).

It is important to bring your baby's temperature down gradually, as a sudden drop in temperature can also cause issues. Keep taking your baby's temperature regularly, and contact your GP if the fever persists or gets worse.

Vomiting

No doubt your sweet little cherub has yakked all down your front by now. It's to be expected – which, incidentally, doesn't make it either pleasant or right. If you're lucky, the puke will go mainly over your in-laws.

Result.

Bringing up a few teaspoons of sick (known as 'possetting') is normal; however, if your baby is constantly vomiting large amounts after each feed, you're best off giving your doctor a call. It could indicate an illness, and will also run the risk of your baby becoming dehydrated.

A vomiting attack can be brought on by a number of things – a car journey, indigestion, or a coughing fit, for example. Whenever I pick Noah up after his feed he tends to hurl a bit of Cow & Gate my way, the little angel.

Excess vomiting in babies should normally pass between 6 to 24 hours after it begins; as long as your baby seems happy and well, there is probably no need to stress. Just keep the fluid intake up and make sure your baby rests, and chances are all will be fine.

Drowsy or Floppy

Bashful, Dopey, Grumpy, Happy, and Doc. Oh, sorry! I thought we were naming dwarfs.

Ten points if you guess the name of this one.

Drowsiness or floppiness in a baby is definitely an indication that something is wrong, and you should seek medical attention quickly.

Rash

Also a good name for a dwarf.

Again, if your baby suddenly develops a rash, or if she has a rash that covers a large area of her body, speak to your GP or health visitor – especially if the rash is accompanied by a fever.

As a parent, the first thing that goes through your mind when you see a rash on your baby is the 'M' word. But meningitis, although serious, is not that common, and has pretty much been on the decline since the late 20th century. However, it's always a good idea to know the warning signs, just in case. So here they are.

- A tense or bulging soft spot
- Fever
- High level of drowsiness
- Vomiting
- Irritable, with a high-pitched or moaning cry
- Fast breathing
- Blotchy skin, getting paler or turning blue
- Extreme shivering
- A stiff body with jerky movements, or a very floppy body
- 'Pin prick' rash/marks or purple bruises on the body
- Cold hands and feet
- Diarrhoea
- Muscle/joint pain

It should be noted that these symptoms are not in order, and not every baby gets all of them. The 'tumbler test' is pretty well known – a meningitis-related rash will not fade when the skin is pressed firmly against a glass.

Bottom line: trust your instincts. If you have any kind of inkling that something is wrong, speak to your GP or head down to A&E immediately.

CHANGING YOUR BABY

That title's pretty misleading. I mean, unfortunately, you are unable to return to the hospital and get a refund for your baby; not even store credit to spend on the cardboard food in the canteen. You can't even exchange your baby for someone else's. Rotters.

Oh, I'm kidding, you'd never want to exchange or return your baby, he's beautiful, of course he is. But that doesn't change the fact that this title could cause some parents to recoil in horror, frantically punch '999' out on the nearest phone and tell the police on me. So let's sort this out, shall we?

CHANGING YOUR BABY'S NAPPY

There we go, now don't sue me.

To be completely honest, there's not a lot I can say about changing your baby's nappy that you don't already know. Short of giving you step-by-step instructions, which would be pretty patronising, I have little to talk about when it comes to your baby's nappy (or 'diaper', if you're American) and its wonderful contents.

However, there is one thing I should tell you. But I can only divulge this information if you promise to keep it a secret.

Studies have shown that men are quicker and more efficient at nappy changing than women.

You may not believe me, but to be honest, I don't really care. It's scientific fact.

"Nursery experts" – as they're described by the *Daily Mail* – have carried out a study of 60 men and women, observing them as they changed the nappy of their stinky baby. They found that while mums lingered over the change, cooing at the child, dads treated the whole thing like more of a 'pit stop' situation, where you get in and get out as quickly as you can before the smell overpowers you and you end up slumped on the floor.

Figure One: Average Nappy Change Times

MEN	WOMEN
1 MIN	2 MIN
36 SECS	5 SECS

That makes us winners, of course, but what is even better is that collectively us dads have decided not to brag about this particular victory and keep it under our hats, instead sitting back smugly as our partners accidentally smear poo all over the carpet.

There's the secret. If you tell anyone, you'll have a lot of angry dads to explain yourself to.

We're listening.

HOW TO DEFUSE AN ATOMIC BOMB

1. Call the Police, MI5, or FBI (USA only).

2. Evacuate the surrounding area.

3. Look at what you're dealing with.

4. Disassemble the detonator.

5. Take apart the elements of the bomb.

6. Prevent toxic levels of radiation by removing all uranium elements.

7. When in doubt, try. Do not be paralysed with fear.

Instructions from associatedcontent.com

how to defuse a soiled nappy

1. Do not call the police, MI5 or FBI. They won't care, unless it's a threat to humanity in general.
2. Yell 'Code Brown!' and evacuate all personnel from the area.
3. Carefully undo any clothing (baby's, that is) and take a look at the damage. If poo is seeping out the sides, that's a bad thing.
4. Remove the nappy with great care, using the front bit to wipe away excess turd. Avoid getting poo on your fingers at all costs.
5. Use nappy wipes or leaves to clean the area of any excess poo.
6. Prevent any additional release of toxic gases by containing the soiled item in a nappy bag.
7. When in doubt, try. Do not be paralysed with fear.

WASHING YOUR BABY

Break out the wax and chamois

It is inadvisable to wash your baby using a hose. Indeed, it'll probably get you into trouble.

Again, as with the last chapter, I'm not going to spend a lot of time jabbering on about how you should wash your kid. You don't need to bath your baby every day, it seems – something which may also rear its smelly head during your child's teenage years – but those in the know at the NHS recommend that you wash his face, neck, hands and bum daily.

"Dude! Put some Lynx on, or something."

Make sure your baby is pretty happy to begin with when you start washing him, as an unhappy baby is just likely to squirm, meaning you won't be able to get the lipstick on him properly. Wait, scratch that. Don't put lipstick on a baby.

You'll need a towel, a nappy, warm water, and cotton wool. Let's wash the little blighter, shall we?

How to Wash Your Baby

Here is a Swedish-looking doll. I will use it to indicate where your baby's various parts are.

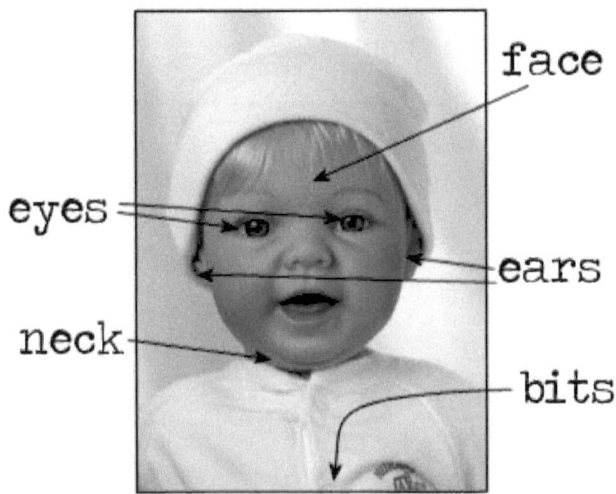

Here's how you wash your baby, according to the Great British National Health Service, who know stuff about things like this.

1. Remove your baby's clothes except for its vest and nappy.
2. Wipe around each eye from the nose outwards, using a fresh piece of cotton wool for each eye.
3. Wipe each ear using new pieces of cotton wool, but don't clean inside the ears.
4. Gently wash your baby's face and neck and pat dry. Do the same for your baby's hands.
5. Take off the baby's nappy. Wash and dry his or her back bottom and front bottom, and put the clean nappy back on.
6. Gently clean around the belly button, if that gross bit of umbilical cord is still attached.

If you've got your head screwed on you may well have realised that those weren't the *exact* words of the NHS. I believe 'front bottom' is not an anatomical term, and that they wouldn't refer to the umbilical cord as 'gross'. But the content is sound.

Bathing Your Baby

This one's got the right idea.

Also, great album.

Bathing your child is simple. There are basically three things you need to remember.

Make sure the water's not too hot.

Try to avoid using any perfumed soaps or shampoo in the first few weeks.

Never leave your baby alone in the water.

Boom! You're done. Now go wash your baby, before I wash it for you. No, wait…I didn't mean that. That's weird. Sorry.

SLEEP AND YOUR BABY

They don't mix.

Before we go any further, I need to get this off my chest. When people say they 'slept like a baby', meaning they had a great night's sleep, they're talking bobbins. If I had a night where I woke up every hour, wet myself frequently and wailed until I was sick, *then* I would count myself as 'sleeping like a baby'. Old people sleep well, normally because they're high on painkillers. Babies, on the other hand, do not sleep.

Glad that's out in the open. I should warn you about something, though: there will, inevitably, be a time in the first few months of your baby's life when a smug mum sidles up to you and proudly declares that her little angel is 'sleeping through'. In that case, you have my permission to push her so she falls down.

Unless you're one of the lucky ones, it is highly likely that your newborn will not sleep through the night. Some don't sleep at all, or at least that's what it feels like. I didn't even realise they showed programmes on TV in the middle of the night before I had kids.

They suck.

Unfortunately, I'm not qualified enough or intelligent enough to tell you in this book how you can get your little one sleeping soundly from 7 till 7. Also, I'm not a magician. What I can give you, though, are some facts about babies and sleep, and a chart showing the normal development of a baby's sleep as it grows. You may even get some decent advice, if you're lucky.

Sleep is pretty important for babies, which makes it all the more bemusing that they don't actually do it. Scientists have discovered that some parts of your baby's brain is more active when he's asleep than when he's awake, as his brain organises and sorts out everything that's gone on during the day. Being a baby that's just come into the world must be akin to being an Amish person in Vegas. You need time to work out what the heck's going on.

Baby sleep also helps build the immune system, as well as promoting growth. You may also notice that your baby twitches during unconsciousness, like a boxer who's just had an uppercut from Mohammed Ali; this is all part of his growth and development.

Starting a Routine

Man, the 'R' word. You will hear the word 'routine' a million times in the first few months of being a parent. Other mums and dads will ask if you've got your baby into a routine yet, what his routine is, how his routine is going. Routine, routine, routine.

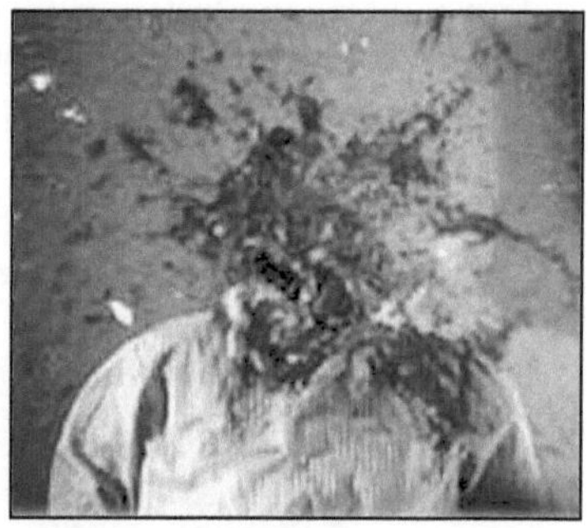

things i think babies dream about

Mind you, they might have a point. Establishing a routine is a great way to help your baby get to sleep quicker and be in the Land of Nod for longer. Here are some tips for you; this actually sounds like an awesome night-time routine, and one I might try myself.

- Give your baby a warm bath, then a decent feed with the lights dimmed.
- Put him in his cot while he's still awake, turn off the lights, and leave him to sleep.
- If your baby stirs and wakes up in the night, don't go in straight away – he may settle of his own accord.
- If he doesn't settle down, go in to him and calm him down. Don't pick him up or talk to him too much. You could sing, but it may make things worse.

A good tip is to avoid rocking your baby to sleep and then putting him down. It'll freak him out if he wakes up in a different place to that in which he fell asleep – which makes sense. I know I'd be spooked if I went to sleep in my bed and woke up in the middle of a field with a cow licking my face.

So how much sleep should your baby be getting? Various boffins who have studied this have come up with a chart showing the 'normal' amount of daytime and night time sleep that a baby should have. You'll notice I've put the word 'normal' in inverted commas, as chances are your baby won't follow this schedule. By the time your child starts school, naps in the day should be a thing of the past; but as you and I both know, once you start work,

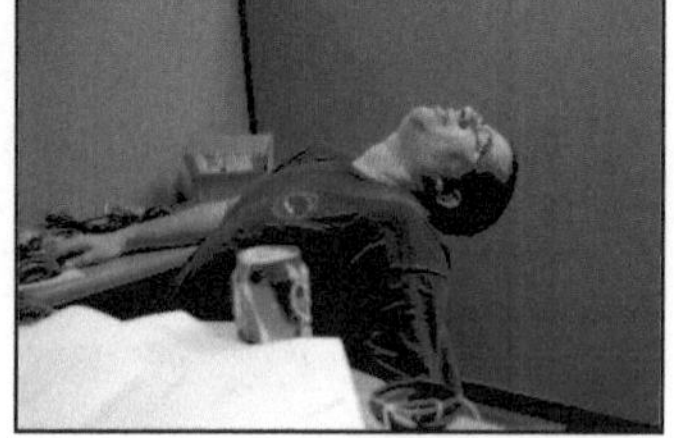

having a snooze at your desk is practically a daily occurrence.

Baby Sleep Chart

The figures in brackets indicate the number of naps in the day that your child should have. Again, don't get too hung up on this – every baby is different.

Age	Night time Sleep	Daytime Sleep	Total Sleep
1 month	8 ½	7 (3)	15 ½
3 months	10	5 (3)	15
6 months	11	3 ¼ (2)	14 ¼
9 months	11	3 (2)	14
12 months	11 ¼	2 ½ (2)	13 ¾
18 months	11 ¼	2 ¼ (1)	13 ½
2 years	10 ½	2 (1)	13
3 years		1 ½ (1)	12

Courtesy of babycenter.com

There are loads of methods that you can use to help your baby sleep through the night – whether it be controlled crying, rocking to sleep, or something else, each has its own advantages and disadvantages. You may not even decide to follow a method, instead choosing to go with the flow. Here's the down-low on a few sleep training methods. (That was me attempting to sound cool).

Baby Sleep Training Methods

Experts and people in the know about things like this say that if you are going to adopt a sleep training method, you should do so from about three months. For the first few weeks after birth, your baby is going to be waking up regularly for feeds, so there's no point even trying to train him to sleep through – although it might be wise to try to implement a routine (there's that word again).

Normally, from three months onwards, a baby has developed a regular sleeping/waking pattern and are capable of sleeping for about five or six hours through the night.

Which different methods of training are there?

I'll tell you, random questioner. There are two main schools of thought when it comes to sleep training methods: 'Cry it Out' and 'No More Tears' (incidentally, two things you don't really want to be saying on a first date or on your wedding night). It is recommended that if you find a method that works for you, you should stick with it to give yourself the best chance of succeeding.

The 'Cry it Out' Method

This train of thought says that it is OK to leave your baby to cry for a bit when he or she is put down to bed. You may choose to leave him to cry for as long as it takes for him to drop off, or you might only let him cry for a set period of time: basically, if it involves letting your baby cry, it falls under this heading.

The bloke in the know when it comes to this method is Richard Ferber, who suggested that a baby crying is an unavoidable part of sleep training.

He also looks vaguely like the KFC guy.

In fact, this guy has become so synonymous with this method of sleep training that you may hear it referred to as 'Ferberisation'. I might come up with a theory or something, and suggest that it's known as 'Wakelingisation'. No, that just sounds stupid. Back to the drawing board.

The thinking behind this method is that your baby will learn to fall asleep on his own, without you having to rock him to sleep – saving you valuable time and giving you much-needed freedom while teaching your baby how to be more independent. If your baby learns to put himself to sleep, Ferber states, he is more likely to soothe himself if he wakes in the night.

That is the main focus of this method: to help your baby to teach himself how to get to sleep, without your help. The crying is simply an inevitable consequence of the learning process.

How do I Ferberize my child?

Just a quick thing: Ferberize should not be confused with Febreze, which is a 'fabric refresher' that stops your sofas smelling like dogs and tobacco. Don't spray your child with Febreze, you'll get arrested.

Here's how you train your child under a 'Cry it Out' method, as helpfully published by those clever bods at BabyCenter.com:

1. Put your baby down in his cot while he's sleepy but still awake.
2. Leave the room. If he cries, let him do so for a set amount of time.
3. Go back into the room to soothe and reassure your baby. Keep your voice quiet and soothing,

but don't pick him up. After a minute, leave the room, even if he's still crying.

4. Stay out of the room for longer than you did the first time. Slowly increase these periods of time between visits to your baby in order to reassure him.
5. Carry on with this routine until your baby's asleep. If he wakes up, repeat steps 3 and 4.
6. The next night increase the amount of time you stay out of your baby's nursery before going in to comfort him.
7. After a few days, you should notice your baby going to sleep on his own.

As far as the set time period goes, the Ferberator (as I'm now calling him) suggests the following:

First Night: Leave for 3 minutes the first time, 5 minutes the second time and ten minutes for any subsequent times.
Second Night: Leave for 5 minutes, then 10, then 12.
Following Nights: Make the intervals longer on each subsequent night.

That's the plan, anyway. Your baby might sleep through almost immediately, or it could be months before he sleeps well. What you should prepare for is the fact that you probably won't sleep much at all.

The 'No More Tears' Method

Some parents may not want to leave their baby to cry; especially the mums, whose maternal hormones will be coursing through her veins every time her little one begins to whinge. You may think that leaving your baby to cry is cruel, unkind, and promoting negative associations with bedtime and sleep. If this is the case, a 'No More Tears' method might be right up your street.

There are a number of well-known baby sleep experts that are big supporters of the 'No More Tears' training method. William Sears is one of the big names associated with 'No More Tears', as well as Elizabeth Pantley.

Elizabeth's the one on the right.

Tips on Achieving the 'No More Tears' Method

Here's a few handy pointers to help you achieve a sleeping training strategy that involves as few tears as possible.

1. Make sure your baby eats a fair amount during the day. It'll help him to identify night-time as sleep time and will stop him from waking up as much in the night.
2. Establish a decent nap schedule in the daytime. This will prevent your baby from becoming over-tired.
3. Put your baby to bed relatively early: around half six to 7pm.
4. Stick to a relaxing bedtime routine, such as a bath, a lullaby, then bed.
5. Repeat a particular phrase to your baby when putting him down to sleep – even something as

simple as saying "sshhh" will indicate to your child that it's time he went to sleep.

6. Make sure all sheets are soft and cosy, and that the temperature of the room is comfortable. Some babies may require complete darkness, some might be alright with the light of a streetlamp coming in through their window.

What else can I say? Whichever method you choose, or even if you don't bother with a method, I hope your baby isn't waking you up too much. I say waking you up: I mean prompting you to pretend to be asleep as you listen to the mrs get up to him. (Cue evil cackle.)

No two babies are the same, though, unless they're identical twins, in which case they are exactly the same. But you know what I mean. What works for one baby may not work for another. Your job is to identify what your baby responds to and stick with it. In the meantime, catch as many 'Z's as you can. Goodness knows you'll be needing them.

FEEDING AND WEANING

Your nipples are useless, stupid.

This isn't the place where I talk about the advantages and disadvantages of breastfeeding and bottle feeding, although it'd be the perfect chapter to do it in. In fact, I've already made this comparison in 'Goodbye, Pert Breasts', so you'll be able to get some good advice there. What do you mean, you haven't bought it? Are you an idiot?

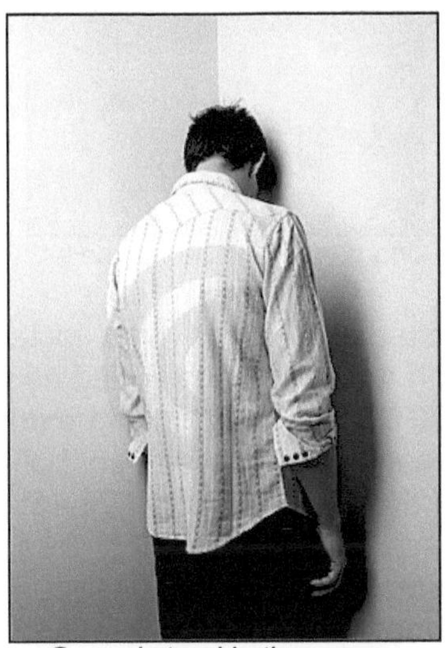

Go and stand in the corner.

There are various pieces of advice that fly around concerning breastfeeding. As I write this, some scientist bods at the Institute of Child Health have recommended that a child should be weaned at four months, instead of six. Argh! Panic! Quick, get that nipple out of your baby's mouth! (Not *your* nipple, obviously. Yours won't work.)

Y'know, I feel sorry for womenfolk of yore who didn't have bright sparks like those bods at the ICH, or the World Health Organisation. I hear mothers in Tudor times panicked and breastfed their children until they were in their mid-60s – in fact, Henry VIII died choking on his mother's teat.

Why d'you think he was so fat?

Mothers in medieval times who lactated through their sackcloth tunics were branded as witches, and dunked in the nearest pond for an extended period of time. Roman women were so baffled by their breasts that they just pistol-whipped their babies across the face, first with the left breast, then with the right, for ten minutes. That's fact. You can use that in conversation. [citation needed]

But seriously, ten years ago the WHO (who?) were telling all mums that the right thing to do was breastfeed for six months. In 2003, the UK adopted this policy. Now, a paper has been published in the British Medical journal stating that six months is too much, and that weaning should begin a couple of months earlier. I predict that in another five years, bespectacled doctors will strongly advise that a newborn baby be "given a steak immediately following birth, preferably medium rare."

So who to believe? Should mothers everywhere burst onto the streets in confusion, bare chested, baby in hand, just looking at their boobs in bemusement, wondering whether they're even required at all?

In my opinion, the fact of the matter is it doesn't matter. What I am quite terribly trying to get across is that women have managed to feed and wean their children for hundreds of years without various bigwigs dishing out advice left, right and centre. You and your mrs know your baby better than anyone else, so just do what feels right for you. If your little guy or girl is developing well, growing properly, and is fit and healthy, then you must be doing something right. So here's Ben's Advice, which I might one day turn into a TV show: breastfeed for as long as you flipping want. (Again, talking mainly to mothers.)

There is a line, of course. Breastfeeding your five year-old is a wee bit freaky, and is bound to draw some rather revolted glances, as well as a page in a national newspaper.

You don't even need to breastfeed at all, if you really don't want to, or can't. Formula milk will do the trick almost as well as breast milk. Heck, I was never breastfed, and I turned out just fine. Kind of.

GRIMMEMENNESKER.DK

Look: this isn't the first time the weaning debate has taken place, and it sure as heck won't be the last. Six months or four months? Booby milk or Cow & Gate? Who knows. For me, though, breast will always be best: but for entirely different reasons.

How Do You Wean a Baby?

Whoa, back up there. That's a big question, like 'What is the meaning of life?' or 'Can you explain *The Matrix Trilogy*?' Let's break this down into bitesize chunks, much like you'll be doing with your baby's food. Gosh, I'm such a wordsmith.

How Do I Know When My Baby's Ready?

There are a few signs to look out for.

Like this one.

Oh, hilarious. If your baby can write, by the way, you should put him on TV. You'll make a fortune.

There are a few suggestions that your baby is ready to be weaned:

- Needing more booby or bottle milk;
- Waking up more often in the night for feeds;
- Taking an interest in food that others in the family are eating;
- Making chewing motions;
- Holding his or her head up and controlling movement;
- Sitting well when supported;
- Trying to put things in his or her mouth.

What Equipment Do I Need?

You can't just pick up food with your fingers and stuff them in your baby's mouth. A few simple items will help make weaning a lot easier – and less messy:

- Plastic spoons – these won't damage your baby's gums if he or she starts chewing them.
- Plastic bowls – you can buy them with a suction pad on the underside, which can help to prevent nasty spills.
- Bibs – your baby will make an almighty mess, and a bib will help to catch at least some of this.
- Ice cube trays – great if you want to freeze small amounts of food.
- Hand blender – you can blend things by hand with this handy hand blender.

With baby food you shouldn't need to sterilise anything after your baby's about six months old, as long as it's well washed. However, make sure you still sterilise any equipment associated with milk, as it's such a great breeding ground for germs.

How to Get Started

So, you're standing in front of your little guy or girl, jar of baby rice in one hand, bottle of formula milk in the other, gripped as if it were some kind of very wet grenade. Across your chest runs a belt of spoons, and on your head is a bowl for a helmet. Man, you look sexy.

When weaning, milk will remain the main source of food for a time; you need to introduce solids gradually, otherwise your child won't get the nutrients required.

1. Begin the meal by feeding your baby milk, as usual.
2. About halfway through, stop and give your baby a little spoonful of food (baby rice is a great start, as it's bland. Fruit and veg puree is also a good idea).
3. Don't worry if your baby gets all confused and spits out the food. Imagine if someone suddenly shoved something weird in your gob when you're halfway through your spag bol.
4. Carry on with the milk.
5. Do the same again the next day, and increase the frequency and amount of feeds as your baby gets more used to it. You want to aim for a solid feed three times a day.

Remember to begin with very fluid food, with no lumps that could pose a choking risk. As time goes on, and your baby develops a chewing action, you can increase the thickness of food and start introducing other foods such as purees of chicken or lean meat, lentils, and baby cereals.

Are There Any Foods to Avoid?

Indeed there are. Vindaloo is one.

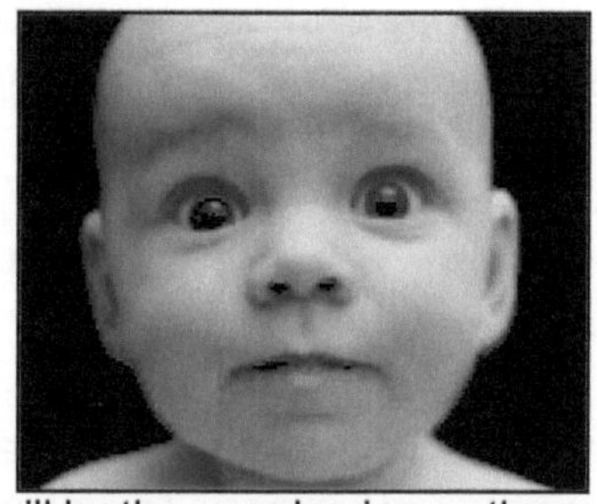

You'll be the one clearing up the mess when it comes out the other end.

Others include:

- Milk – avoid cow's milk until your baby is at least a year old;
- Salt – avoid altogether;
- Sugar – only use in very small amounts, if you have to;
- Eggs – be sure they're cooked thoroughly;
- Honey – wait for at least a year;
- Nuts – for ground nuts, hold off until your child is three years old. For whole and chopped nuts, wait for five years.

If you want to save a bit of time, make up a load of food and freeze it in ice cube trays. You can then defrost as much or as little as you think your baby needs as and when you like.

As your baby grows, you may wish to introduce finger foods, such as sticks of cheese, cooked carrot, bread sticks, and rusks. These are especially great if your baby is teething; but obviously stay nearby, as there is a choking risk where finger foods are involved.

So that's how to wean your baby, in a nutshell. Soon, you'll be sat next to him at the table, critiquing your wife's food to the point where she gets so frustrated you find yourself in a headlock. All part of being a parent, I'm afraid.

how biology ruins boobies

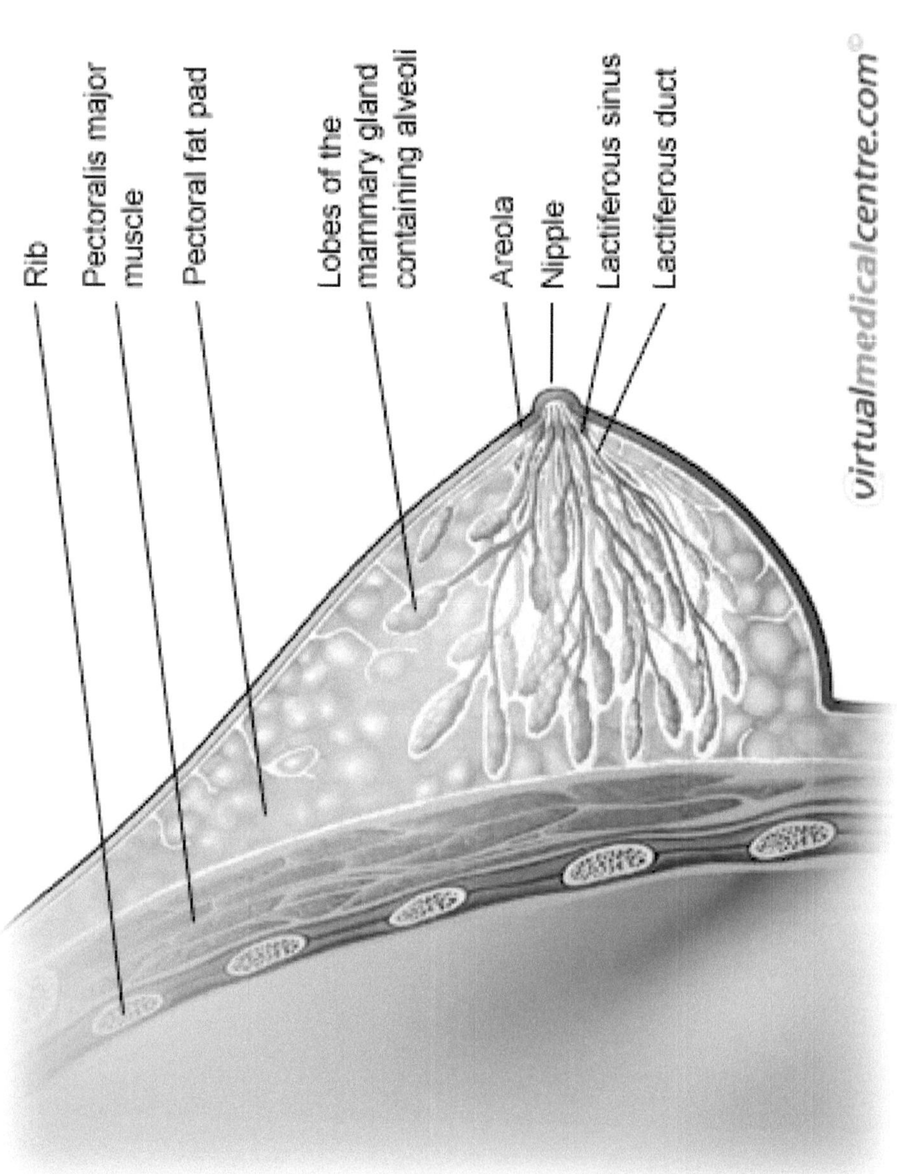

TEETHING

Wouldn't it look weird if only the bottom set grew?

S'funny, isn't it, the circle of life? You're born without teeth, and most old fuddy-duddies die without teeth. The same kind of rule applies for nappies and bladder control.

It's happened again.

When your baby cuts his first gnasher is anyone's guess: it could be as early as three months, or as late as one year. There was even a baby born in Cambridgeshire in 2011 who popped out of the womb proudly showing off two little front incisors – a 1 in 2,500 occurrence.

For many parents, a teething baby can be a pretty stressful time. Anyone who's ever had a wisdom tooth come through knows how painful it is. Well, your baby will be cutting 20 teeth. So man up, for crying out loud. Your baby is harder than you.

What are the Symptoms of Teething?

Teeth.

Oh, LOL. There are a number of signs that your little one might be cutting his first teeth. Your child may get all of these, or just a few, with varying levels of severity. Helpful, aren't I? Bet you're glad you bought this book now.

- Due to the fact that a tiny sharp tooth is carving its way to the surface of your baby's gum, there's a fair chance he'll be pretty **irritable**. This may be worse if the molars are coming in, although you can soothe your child by explaining to him that at least he'll be able to grind food now.
- Your baby might **drool**, much like you do when Anna Kournikova is thrashing around on TV. This excess spittle could cause your baby to **cough**, which I doubt you do when watching scantily-clad women. It's a bit weird if you do.
- This constant drooling can irritate the skin, so you may find that your baby gets a **chin rash**. This can be prevented by gently wiping your baby's face every now and then.
- Your baby will **bite and gnaw** on pretty much anything within reach, so mind your toes.
- You might find that the pain spreads to the ears and cheeks, so **cheek rubbing** and **ear pulling** might be evident, particularly when the molars come in.
- The pain may also mean that your little guy or girl **doesn't sleep well**, which is as sucky for you as it is for him.
- Other symptoms include **diarrhoea** and a **high temperature**, although it's disputed whether these are direct signs of teething.

How Many Teeth Will My Child Grow?

Well, that depends. If you're a hillbilly, you'll be used to having around five.

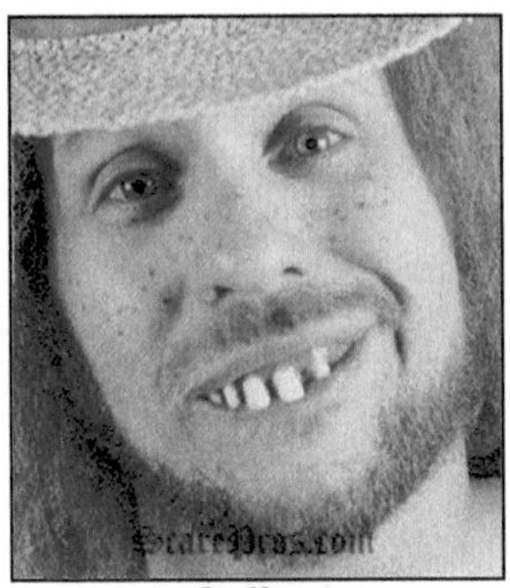

Guffaw.

There's another group of people I've alienated. Sorry about that.

Your baby will have twenty teeth, which will have all come through by the time he or she is around two or three years old. That's twelve teeth less than the average adult, unless you're a hillb- wait, I'm doing it again! Focus, Benjamin.

At around six years of age, your little one's milk teeth will start to fall out, leading to the inevitable school photo when his front two teeth are missing. You know, the photo that spends most of its time face-down on the mantelpiece.

Here's a rough timescale of when your baby's teeth will show their little pearly faces:

Age	Teeth	Position
6-7 months	Central Incisors	Two top, two bottom
7-9 months	Two more incisors	Top and bottom
10-14 months	First molars	Double teeth for chewing
15-18 months	Canines	The 'fangs'
2-3 years	Second molars	The second set of double teeth

Baby Teeth

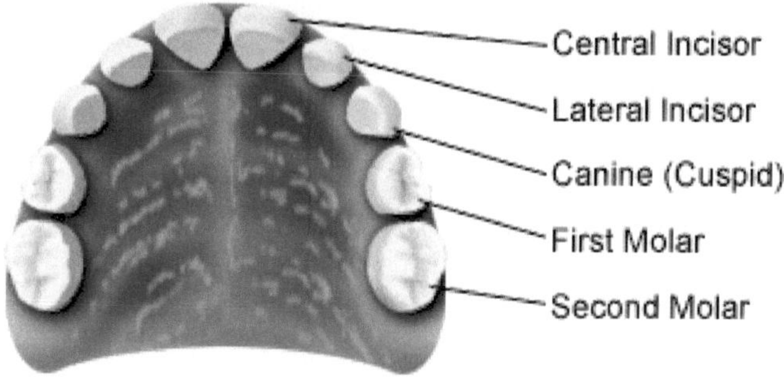

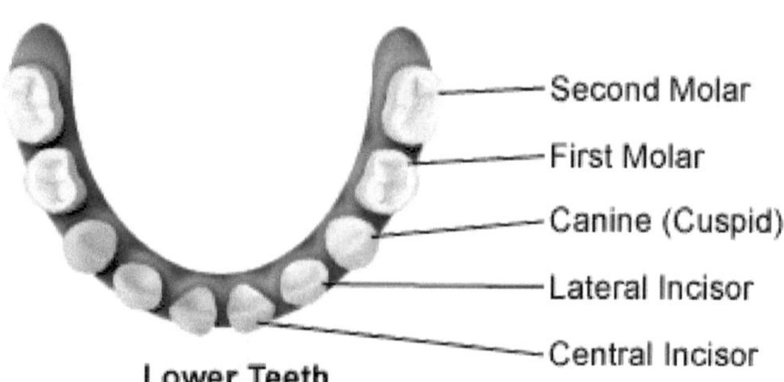

I'm sorry about this picture. It's like a scene from *Jaws*.

How Can I Help With The Pain?

When doing a bit of research on how to help soothe your baby's pain, I stumbled across the following sentence:

> *"There are several things that you can try to help ease the pain of teething; some work and some don't."*

I'm not sure why you'd even try the ones that don't work. It's good to know that there's stuff out there that's even less helpful than the daft whitterings in this book.

There are a bunch of **teething toys** available, all with nice squidgy rings that your baby can gnaw on until it's blue in the face. Anything cold will help numb the pain, such as **chilled water or a bit of pureed fruit** which has been lobbed in the fridge for a bit.

If all else fails, you may want to turn to some **medicine**, such as infant Tylenol or Calpol – which is, by the way, the tastiest medicine ever.

As with all things, if in doubt, have a chat with your GP or health visitor, who may be able to recommend some other remedies for those nasty teething pains. Giving your baby whiskey, although effective (supposedly), is probably illegal.

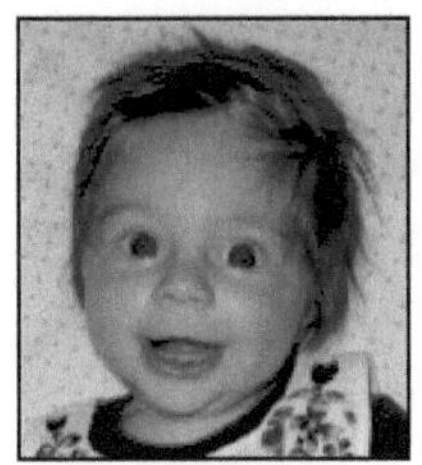

Sozzled.

BABY SIGNING

Flipping the bird from 3 weeks old

Baby signing is a relatively new thing that's swept parents everywhere. But first, a funny photo.

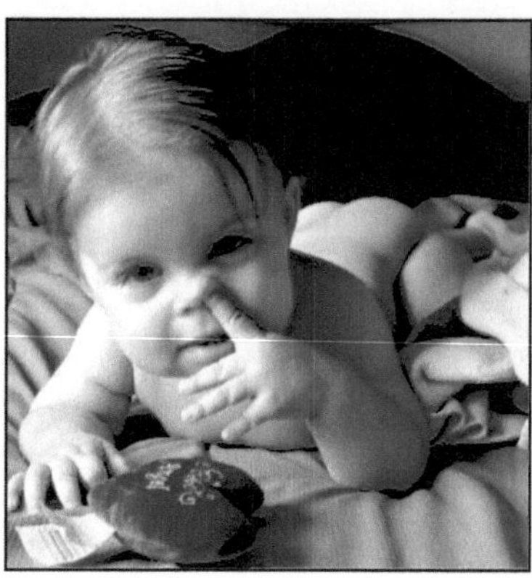

You know how when you're in a meeting, or with some friends, and someone else is talking so much you just can't get a word in? That's how it feels for babies all the time. Their ability to speak lags behind their intelligence in the first few months of life, and so they want to get something across to you but can't because their darn mouths won't move properly.

But hurrah! Their hopes are answered with the advent of baby signing. Don't be fooled, though: your child won't end up gesticulating wildly like those people in the corner of your TV screen, nor will they flip the bird to the drivers of cars that cut you up. Not unless you teach them to, of course.

Baby signing is new-ish, depending on how old you are and the year in which you're reading this book right now. It was first picked up as an idea for baby communication in the early 1980s by a couple of boffin ladies named Linda Acredolo and Susan Goodwyn, university professors and all-round bright sparks.

This was then picked up by a few other clever clogs as time went on, namely a guy named Joseph Garcia in 1986, and Kimberlee Whaley in 1998; and it's risen from there. And hey, guess what? Whaley's research has found that girls use signs more than boys. *Another* thing they're better than us at.

Anyway, all this talk of history is boring, and makes me want to punch myself in the face.

I Googled 'punch self in face' to get this little gem.

Let's get down to the nitty-gritty, which incidentally is what landed you in this role of father to begin with. What are the pros and cons of baby signing, other than being able to talk about your in-laws with your baby without them knowing what's going on?

Advantages first.

If the signing process is slightly tweaked, your baby will be able to throw shapes like Justin Timberlake at the tender age of eight months, although it is highly unlikely that your child will become some kind of international sex symbol because of it.

I jest, of course. There are a number of reported benefits of having a baby who can sign, although there is little in the way of research that proves these definitively. Still, it must be better to have a signing baby than one who just lies there and poops, right?

The most obvious advantage is that it **improves communication** between you and your child. Your baby will be able to tell you if he wants to eat, which will save you the effort of screaming “WHAT DO YOU WANT?!” as you yank out clumps of your own hair while he cries on the floor and wriggles a bit. Other common baby expressions include ‘sleep’, ‘more’, ‘hug’, ‘play’, and even ‘cookie’.

It is suggested that baby signing also **boosts creativity**, as your baby soon realises that a good gesture results in getting what he wants, and therefore learns that expressing himself is a pretty good darn thing to do. This carries on into later life, although mooning someone out of a car window is not considered to be the highest form of creative expression.

Your **baby is happier**, as his needs are met and he has the confidence to be able to communicate to you and others. That’s why he’s smiling creepily at you right now, out of the corner of your eye.

It’s advantageous for you as a parent, too. As well as **saving you time** which would have been spent getting your Inspector Morse on and painstakingly working out what your child wants through a lengthy process of elimination, it also **gives you satisfaction** in allowing you to provide your child with exactly what he wants; unless he signs something like ‘Porsche’, of course.

What about the disadvantages?

You have to scrape the barrel a bit when it comes to listing the cons of baby signing. There may be a bit of a **breakdown in communication** if the person the baby is communicating to doesn’t understand or know the signs, but it’s not like it’s going to lead to neglect or anything, so it’s no big deal.

Another common fear is that a baby who is great at signing will **take longer to talk**, on account of the fact that he can already communicate pretty well with just signs. This is a misplaced fear and, if anything, kids who have learned signing from an early age have shown an **increased vocabulary** as they’ve grown.

That’s pretty much it for disadvantages. I mean, it’s not like anything really bad can come from a simple gesture...can it?

Why you little...!
(grabs Hitler in a headlock)

BABY MASSAGE

No...you have to massage the baby, stupid.

If only babies could give you a massage, eh? It'd help with the stress they cause, at least.

Anyway, while you're pondering the mental image of your baby karate-chopping your shoulders, let's crack on and have a wee chat about baby massage. As with all things, when you're researching something, you head to Wikipedia (I know, I know, it's not reliable, but if you think I'm trawling the pages of the *British Medical Journal* you can go swivel).

Here's what Wikipedia has to say about infant massage:

"Infant massage is massage..."

Good start.

"...given to a young infant..."

I can feel my brain growing with all this knowledge.

"...to enhance their cognitive and physical development. Such contact is also found in other mammals where the mother provides tactile stimulation as part of their care through ***licking, grooming*** *and physical contact."*

Ha! Imagine licking your baby as part of a decent massage. Like, right across the back of his head. How weird.

I'm sorry. It's late, and I'm struggling. Shall we talk a bit more about baby massage?

Start with the advantages.

Not just beneficial for 'full term' infants, baby massage has been proven to help **preterm infants gain more weight** than those who do not receive any massaging. These babies also showed increased bone mineralization, density, length and head circumference. They **sleep better**, and show higher **motor development**.

The same goes for babies born at full term, **reducing irritability** and **reducing crying**. It's even good for mums with postnatal depression, with research by the Foetal and Neonatal Stress Research Group showing that it can **reduce PND**, **improve your bond with your baby**, and **help you both relax**.

Baby massage can also **ease medical problems**, such as colic, constipation and wind, and you may find that you let off a little guff of your own during the massage process; although it would rather kill the mood.

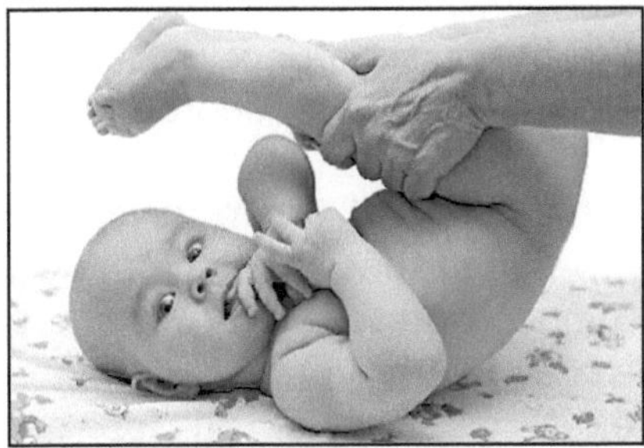

Frrrt.

Any Disadvantages?

No. Stop being negative. Just remember not to press too hard, and everything will be fine.

How do I massage a baby?

Your baby, you mean. You can't just go massaging anyone's baby. There are laws against that kind of thing.

Getting the Mood Just Right

As with any massage, it's important that the atmosphere is just right to help maximise relaxation.

Get some **massage oil**. Be careful when choosing an oil, as some can irritate your baby's skin – plus, you don't want to run the risk of them ingesting any potentially harmful substances. The best oil to use is sesame oil, but you can use olive oil as well. It just means your kid will smell like chips.

Make sure the **room is warm and quiet**, as your baby will be stripped of his clothing and won't relax much if he gets all cold and ends up looking like a raw chicken. Similarly, if you've got Iron Maiden screeching in the background, your kid is going to get stressed; not least because Iron Maiden suck.

Get something **soft and warm** for your baby to lie on, but bear in mind that your little one may decide to relax too much and wee everywhere, so be sure to include a waterproof covering in there somewhere. A thick towel on top of a plastic changing mat will do the trick.

Make sure you choose the right **time** to massage your child – in between meals so he's not too hungry, or late at night when he's too tired. You also need to make sure you're as relaxed as possible, as your baby will sense if you're tense.

Move aside, Shakespeare. I'm the new poet in town.

Many baby massage tutors also tell you to ask your baby's permission to massage it before you get going. It seems a bit odd to me, but I suppose at least your baby will be able to use his newly-acquired gift for signing to tell you to shove off if he doesn't fancy it.

Another tip - if you're unsure as to how much pressure to use - is to close your eye and press your finger on your eyelid, making sure you stop before it feels uncomfortable. That's about the same pressure you should use on your baby.

Gentle Strokes, Gentle Strokes

Here are the different strokes you can use when massaging your baby. Some of them have funny names, but grow up, you blithering idiot.

Milking

Snigger.

This move (we're calling them 'moves' now) is used on the arms and legs. Start at the top of the limb and move it down to the wrist or ankle, squeezing gently. Imagine you're milking a cow, or, if that's too weird, pretend you're squeezing the filling out of a sausage. Mind you, that's also pretty weird. As one hand reaches the wrist or ankle, start at the top with the other hand so that there's a continuous effect.

Weird.

Open Book

This move is used on your baby's chest, back and forehead. This is slightly more complicated than simply milking your child's legs, so pay attention.

Place your palms together in a praying gesture, place your little fingers against your baby's skin and 'open the book' by spreading your hands until your thumbs reach the baby's flesh. Move your hands outward across your baby's skin in a smooth motion.

Please note that this move doesn't involve an *actual* book. Your baby will not be amused if you sandwich it between a copy of *War and Piece* and *Harry Potter*.

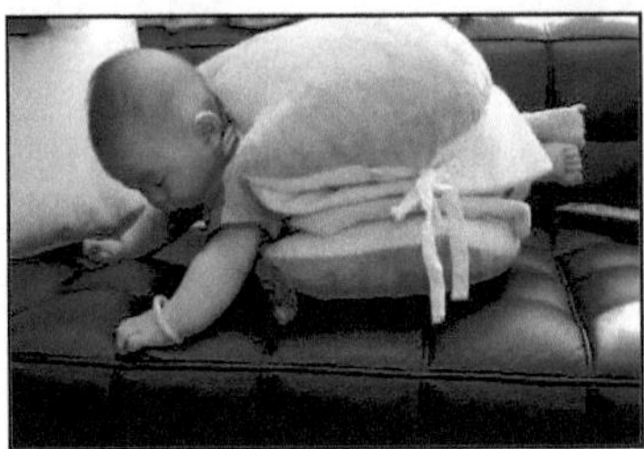

Although a baby sandwich isn't a bad idea.

Rolling

Don't roll over your baby! That *is* a bad idea.

Rolling is used on your baby's arms and legs, and is a pretty common massage move. Place your non-writing hand under the limb and your other hand on top. Roll the limb between the hands, moving your main hand in circles and moving it slowly down the limb.

Use these strokes five times each when massaging your baby, and in no time you'll have the most chilled out child in the history of mankind. I suggest the following sequence:

1. Open Book
2. Roll
3. Milk
4. Roll
5. Bake
6. Knead
7. Simmer
8. Drain
9. Spread
10. Cool for 2 mins

MILESTONES

Don't freak if your baby doesn't develop at the same rate as this chart. We're all different. I still can't hold a spoon properly.

One Month

- Lifts head
- Responds to sound
- Stares at faces

Two Months

- Vocalises sounds – gurgling, etc.
- Follows objects
- Holds up head for short periods of time

Three Months

- Laughs
- Holds head steady
- Recognises your face

Four Months

- Holds head steadily for long periods of time
- Can bear weight on legs
- Makes sounds when you talk to him

Five Months

- Distinguishes between bold colours
- Can roll over
- Can sit up for short periods of time
- Amuses himself by playing with his hands and feet

Six Months

- Turns towards sounds and voices
- Imitates sounds, blows bubbles

Seven Months

- Sits up without support
- Reaches for things
- Imitates speech sounds (babbles)

Eight Months

- Says 'dada' and 'mama' to either parent
- Begins to crawl
- Passes objects between hands

Nine Months

- Combines syllables into word-like sounds
- Stands while holding on to something

Ten Months

- Waves goodbye
- Picks up things with a pincer grasp
- Crawls
- Pulls himself around objects while standing

Eleven Months

- Says 'dada' and 'mama' to the right parent
- Stands on his own for a couple of seconds

Twelve Months

- Imitates others' activities
- Jabbers word-like sounds
- Indicates wants with gestures

Information from babycentre.co.uk

SECTION TWO

INFANT

(12 months – 3 years)

Oh my word, he's moving. Not as in the 'lying-on-his-back-kicking-his-legs' moving, I mean *actually moving around.* This means that I can't just lie him on the floor with a load of toys at five in the morning and have a quick snooze on the sofa, safe in the knowledge that he's not going anywhere. Now I have to stay awake and keep an eye on him, or I'll wake up and he'll have somehow managed to trap himself inside the chest of drawers.

These few years are some of the most exciting in your child's life, as well as yours. Every day he or she will do something that will amaze and astound you: stringing words together in a sentence, going to the loo by himself, that kind of thing. Y'know, all things that you can do perfectly well, yet no-one congratulates you for.

So, brace yourself for another three years on the fatherhood rollercoaster. Just try not to yak everywhere.

THE IMPORTANCE OF MAKING FRIENDS

Because if you don't, people will mock you.

Now your kid is a bit older, your mrs will probably start taking him (or her) to playgroups. Taking your child to these kinds of events will inevitably prompt kicking, screaming and perhaps a bit of crying.

(Wait for it…inevitable punchline approaching…)

…and that's just you.

Genius. But yes, you will undoubtedly get dragged along to one of these playgroup things, where you spend an hour or two knee-deep in screaming kids

THE MANY FACES OF A DAD WHEN HE GETS ROPED INTO GOING TO A BABY PLAYGROUP, INCIDENTALLY NOT UNLIKE THE FIVE STAGES OF GRIEF

DENIAL

"This ain't happening to me, so rod off."

ANGER

"NOOOOOOOOOOOOOO!!"

BARGAINING

"I will wash up every day for
two months...
THREE MONTHS!"

DEPRESSION

sigh

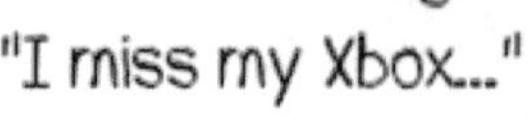

"I miss my Xbox..."

ACCEPTANCE

"Ain't no point in arguing anyway,
just think about the footy..."

and nattering mums whilst wishing you were face-deep in a pint somewhere.

I've been there, friend. You wade through a swamp of children, taking care not to step on any chubby limbs, and take the one vacant plastic chair of the many that run around the edge of the room. Mums huddle together in their gaggles, bitching and gossiping, every now and then looking over their shoulder to eye up the male that has dared enter their lair.

And they don't look anything like this.

If you look around, though, you'll notice you're not on your own. Dotted about the room will be other parents (maybe even some dads) who are sat alone, Billy No-Mates, suffering flashbacks to the school prom when they were also sat on their tod. Now and again your eyes will meet, and you'll share some kind of lonely camaraderie.

But it doesn't *have* to be quite so terrible. In fact, playgroups are a great place to make some new friends. Adult friends, I mean. If parents see you having a good old chat with their child they might think you are a tad strange.

How do I make friends?

Crumbs, you sound so lonely. Man up.

The thing to remember is this: adults are a lot different from kids. When you were at school and wanted to join a group, you'd approach their little huddle and linger around the perimeter for a bit. If you were lucky, you could wriggle your way between a couple of people, engage in a bit of conversation –and, before you knew it, you'd have some mates.

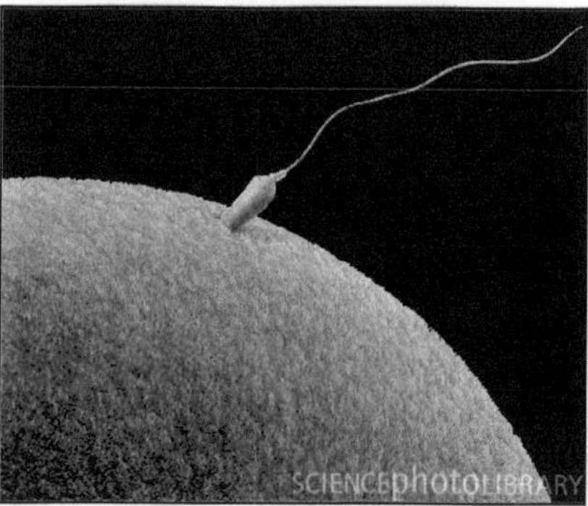

By the way, the whole 'wriggling into the group' thing bears striking similarities to fertilisation.

This didn't always happen, of course, and – for me, at least – nine times out of ten you'd get a wedgie and your lunch money nicked. Fortunately, this rarely happens at parent-toddler playgroups. I've only ever seen it done once or twice.

The trick to finding someone to talk to – assuming you want to, of course – is to let your child waddle off into the maze of toys and see who he plays with. Identify the parent of the other kid, and Boom! You've got yourself a conversation starter.

OK, I'm sat next to them now. What do I talk about?

You really want me to spoon-feed you, don't you?

Talk about kids, for a start. It's the one thing you have in common, assuming the other person isn't childless and simply there to gawp at toddlers.

Chat about their kid more than your kid, asking how old they are, what they like to do, that kind of thing. Other parents just love to talk about their kids, so asking about them is a sure-fire winner.

Ask for some advice, if you *really* want to make the other person feel good and therefore like you more. It could be about how to get your kid to sleep, or to play better with others, whatever: as long as you're requesting that they spill out their boundless knowledge to you, you've got 'em by the short and curlies.

What else can we talk about?

Here are some topics of conversation you can instigate.

- The latest news and sport
- Local events
- The economy
- Your bowel movements
- What breed of dog you think you could beat in a bare-knuckle fight if you were naked
- Genital puppetry
- How soft their cervix is (restricted to women only)
- The official rules of Baby Wrestling
- Conspiracy theories about the moon landings

WHAT TO DO WHEN A TODDLER YOU DON'T KNOW COMES UP TO YOU AND DRIBBLES ALL OVER YOUR JEANS

Do I need to make parent friends?

Not unless you enjoy sitting on your own.

Now you're a parent, you see, you will probably eventually find yourself partying with the lads less and less, and going to soft play centres more and more. Whilst there's nothing wrong with just you and your little guy or girl going on your own, it'll be great for your child's development and social skills to run around these places with a friend or two.

If your child plays regularly with another kid of the same age, it will promote the development of their imagination and interaction skills, as well as keeping them fit and healthy. Make sure they enjoy it while it lasts; before long your child will be a teenager, and all of these skills will be lost in a sea of grunting, slouching and thinking you're 'sad'.

This is what we've got to look forward to.

ENCOURAGING YOUR CHILD TO WALK

Because slapping your thighs and squeaking "C'mon" has limited success

Everyone gets really hung up on when their kid should be sitting up, or crawling, or walking, or whatever, which is a bit hypocritical for me to say as I put that 'Milestones' bit in a few pages back. Soz.

It's true, though. My wife and I found ourselves beginning to panic when Noah wasn't sitting up by himself at six months. We had visions of him never learning how, and slipping off chairs during business meetings when he's 30.

"Uhh, guys? I'm slipping…"

This anxiety worsens when you see babies whose belly buttons have barely gone all crusty swaggering around playgroups like they own the place.

Comparing your child's progress to that of other kids is a pointless game, but it's one that as human beings in the 21st century we can't help but do. So if your kid isn't walking when the dates tell you he should be, don't sweat it. Also, avoid attaching strings to his limbs and making him walk via the magic of puppetry.

Stop being daft. What can I do to help?

Sorry. There are some things that you can do to encourage your child to take his first steps. And here they are.

As with all things, infants need practice when learning how to walk. It would be unreasonable to expect your child to suddenly raise himself up on his hind legs one day, dust off his hands, and stride out of the room. Although it would be a pretty epic moment.

For an infant to walk, he needs legs that are capable of supporting his body weight. This may seem like a pretty obvious thing to say, but if your baby's getting carried around all the time he's never going to use his legs, and they will become weak. Some infants' legs are actually too muscular, which can affect balance and cause problems with walking.

Can't work out if this is cute or disturbing.

Encourage your child to stand up on his or her own by putting his favourite toys on a low table and lifting him up so he can reach them. Make sure his legs are taking his weight, and gradually release your grip until you are lightly holding his waist.

Your child may be so distracted that he stands there for a while, until he figures out what's going on and falls over. It's similar to when your dad used to tell you he was pushing you when you took the stabilisers off your bike for the first time. You'd suddenly discover that actually you were cycling under your own steam, panic, and throw yourself off the saddle.

"You LIEEEED to MEEE!!"

Once your little lad or lady becomes more confident standing up, line up some chairs against a wall. Put a toy on the last chair, and encourage your child to 'cruise' towards it – grabbing onto the chairs and pulling himself along.

Before you know it, your child will be legging it about, running into doors and walls and generally making you wish you'd never taught him in the first place. Funny how life has a habit of biting you in the ass, eh?

LEARNING TO SPEAK

So they can repeat everything you say to the person you said it about

"Why?"

The very sound of the word makes you clench your teeth and bumcheeks as you stare angrily into the middle distance.

"Because it does, that's why."

Pause.

"But why?"

Snap.

"I don't KNOW why, OK?! It just stands on one leg because that's what flamingos do, alright? Now zip it!"

You'll soon learn, if you haven't already, that the novelty soon wears off when your kid learns something new. Take speaking for example: one minute, you're like "Oh, *listen!* He's *talking!*" Then, you're all like "Oh, *great*. He's *talking.*"

But hey, learning how to speak is all part of growing up – and it *is* great when your child says your name for the first time. It's not so great when they mimic your swearing in front of your grandparents.

There are certain things that you can do to encourage speaking, which can be found overleaf.

most common first words

"da-da"
"car"
"mamma"
"cat"
"woof"
"ball"
"apple"
"decubitis"
"witzelsucht"
"macrologist"
"gressible"

When is my kid going to speak?

Chances are, your child is already speaking, and has been from a couple of months old: it's just you can't understand what he's saying, like when politicians talk.

I know this section is from 12 months to 3 years, but let's start at the beginning and take a look at your child's developing communication.

1-3 months

Babies only really communicate for the first three months of their life by crying at you, often in the middle of the night. They can smile at you, which makes things better for about ten seconds, after which they'll undoubtedly change their mind and continue crying.

4-5 months

During this phase of your baby's life, he or she will start making cooing sounds, often when they're happy about something. Any words formed at this stage is probably just a fluke – either that, or your baby's a freakin' genius.

6-9 months

A six month-old baby will respond to his name, although in a sweet way, and not in the "WHAAAAT?!" that you'll undoubtedly get during your sweet one's teenage years. Common words at this stage are 'da-da', 'mamma', and 'no'. Your child may recognise what 'yes' and 'no' mean.

10-12 months

A child in this phase of development will be able to relate the words 'da-da' and 'mamma' to you and your mrs, and can understand a lot of what you say. They will undoubtedly have a larger vocabulary, which basically consists of demanding stuff from you.

1-3 years

Your child will now be able to use increasingly complex sentences, and you can have proper conversations – which, again, will mostly consist of him demanding things. His vocabulary will expand daily, and he will begin to mimic what you say – so avoid bitching about the in-laws within earshot.

How can I encourage my child to speak?

It may come as a surprise to you that your two month-old child doesn't understand a word you're saying; which is why, when you are talking to your baby, you should use high-pitched, singsong tones that make you sound like a simpering idiot. This will keep your baby interested and make the connection between what he hears and the sounds that come out of his mouth.

When your kid is a bit older, at around 8 months, you can read to him. Again, he won't understand the words, but the brightly coloured pictures will stimulate his senses and help promote a bond between you and your baby. The illustrations, of course, depend on what you're reading.

Having a good sing to your baby is also great for introducing different sounds to your child. You can blast out a bit of Limp Bizkit, perhaps, or croon in his face like Michael Bublé. You can even dabble in a bit of Celine Dion, if you really want to; although other people may judge you if you start warbling in the middle of a crowded room.

When your baby is this age, a great thing to do is simply to mimic what your baby says. Be warned: you'll find yourself having half-hour long conversations with your child that consist of nothing but babbling and a bit of dribble.

By the time your child is about 16 months old, he or she will have a vocabulary of about 50 words – much the same as your average football lout.

"Kick that - round thing…over in that!" *(dribbles)* "Ooooooyyy!"

When you're reading books with your child, try to elaborate on things, as well as talking about the illustrations. This will help beef up your baby's vocabulary. A good tip is to wait for your child to tell you when he wants something, such as a refill or a toy – it'll prompt him to use his own words to communicate.

Once your kid is stringing together his first sentences, you can encourage him by asking him questions about the story you're reading. "Why *did* the cow jump over the moon?" is one question, although I'm not sure I really know the answer. Drugs, perhaps?

Ask him to tell you what he's done during the day, and elaborate on each point to encourage him to be more descriptive. Be careful not to push it, though – if your child feels he is struggling to communicate he could get upset.

I suppose it *is* great, really, that your child is asking so many questions, because it just shows he's trying to learn. But there are times when I find honesty is the best policy – and is great at shutting them up. Take being at the zoo, for example, to link in with the little dialogue thing I had going on at the start of the chapter:

> *"Daddy, what's that?" (points)*
>
> *Dad looks.*
>
> *"That, son, is an elephant's willy."*
>
> *Kid gapes, Dad swaggers off.*

Heck yeah.

POTTY TRAINING

Same poo, different location

Unfortunately, somewhere in between starting life in a nappy and ending life in a larger nappy, we have to learn how to don our tighty whities and do our business in the loo and not on the move. Why can't someone just pass a law saying that we have to wear nappies our whole life?

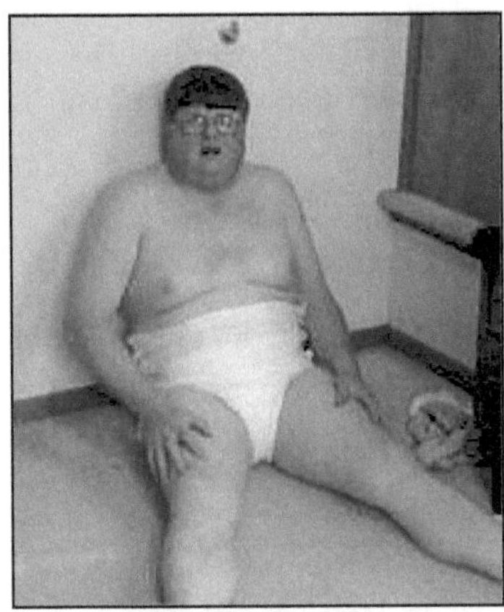

Oh. That's why.

At some point during your child's life you're going to need to start potty training him, otherwise he'll be on the loo at work yelling for someone to wipe his bottom, or squatting over a potty next to his desk.

Alright, shut up, let's get flippin' serious, and do some quick-fire questions.

When should I start potty training my child?

Any time between 18 and 32 months, although – as always – each child is different.

How do I know if my child is ready to be trained?

Signs to look out for include walking to the potty and undressing, prolonged periods of nappy dryness, and letting you know that he or she needs to go to the loo.

How long will potty training take?

Three to twelve months, usually, although it all depends, blah blah blah. Your child will probably be fully independent when it comes to toilet time between the ages of two and a half and four – in fact, 80% of children are completely trained by the age of three and a half.

If my child can't easily master potty training, does that mean he's thick?

Don't be daft. There is no correlation between how long it takes a child to adapt to something and future skills or intelligence.

What's the best potty to use?

You'll find that your child will prefer either a potty chair or one of those toilet seats. Isaac, my firstborn, hated using the potty but felt like a 'big boy' when using the loo.

How often do toddlers wee during the day?

A bit of an odd question, but we'll crack on nonetheless. Most children pee four to eight times a day, roughly every two hours.

...and poo?

Weird. But once or twice a day. By the time it comes to potty training your child, you'll have probably noticed a pattern regarding the frequency and timing of bowel movements.

Anything else I should know?

- Girls tend to start training earlier and complete it quicker than boys. Again.
- Think about setting up a reward system to provide an incentive for your child.
- Practice being patient – you'll need it.
- Make sure your child is wearing clothes that can easily be pulled down in times of desperation.
- Night-time training tends to be more difficult: 25% of five year-olds still wet the bed. Pull-ups are a good way of staving off sopping sheets.
- Never force your child to sit on the loo, or hold him down on one until he's done a wee.
- Never tell your child off if he has an accident, but always cheer like an idiot when he does it right.
- There are five words which will send a chill down your spine every time they are uttered…

HOW TO DEAL WITH TEMPER TANTRUMS

Your child's, not your own...

...although I've seen you strop, and it's pretty darn funny. Your voice goes all high-pitched, and your face screws up like a scrotum.

Anyway, enough about you. At some point your child will start having temper tantrums.

Get used to this face.

The risk is that this can happen anywhere, at any time, much like a heart attack or the realisation your fly's been undone all day. We've all seen it: a parent standing all exasperated in the frozen foods aisle in Asda, as her kid writhes and screams on the floor because he was told he couldn't have an ice cream.

When it happens to someone else, it's great. You can step over the child with a little smirk on your face, safe in the knowledge that it isn't your kid, as well as comforted by the fact that other children strop as badly as yours do.

You need some ammo, in the form of knowing what to do when your child starts shrieking like a banshee, veins popping and whatnot.

First of all, you need to know your enemy. Yes, that's right, in this little skit your child is the enemy. Now pay attention. We're entering:

TANTRUM BOOT CAMP

Codename: Operation Shut the Heck Up

The Enemy: Your child
Objective: Neutralising temper tantrums

Your objective is to minimise the threat of a tantrum occurring, and - in the event of said tantrum - deal with it in such a way that old ladies don't tut at you as they hobble by and you don't look like some kind of abuser.

Likelihood of Conflict
High. The enemy will tend to have his/her worst tantrums between the ages of 1 and 4 - and, for once, girls are just as bad as boys.

Reasons for Conflict
There are a number of reasons why the enemy chooses to indulge in a temper

tantrum. Knowing the reasons why this happens gives you valuable intelligence, and can help defuse an otherwise volatile situation.

- **Frustration:** If the enemy is struggling to communicate or cannot make you understand their needs, you may find yourself on the sticky end of a hissy fit.
- **Independence:** Your child - I mean, the enemy - may see simple things as a threat to his/her independence, and go off on one.
- **Hunger/Tiredness:** This breeds irritability, which can cause a highly unstable and explosive environment.
- **Refusal:** Perhaps the main cause of tantrums, refusing the enemy access to or possession of something will almost certainly light the temper fuse.
- **Attention:** Your child, like you, craves attention. If he doesn't get it he will, like you, throw a fit.

Neutralising the Threat of Tantrums

With practice and timing, the threat of conflict can be neutralised before it boils over into a full-blown tantrum. This can be achieved through a few processes:

- **Setting an Example:** The enemy is less likely to explode if you keep your cool when other skirmishes or problems arise. Diplomacy is the key to peace, as well as plenty of nice food.

Praise: Encourage and reward good behaviour. Punish bad behaviour using a variety of means at your disposal - avoiding hand-to-hand combat, of course.

Diversion: Using diversionary tactics when you spot conflict bubbling is a good way of avoiding an all-out clash.

Offer Choice: Allow the enemy to make his/her own decisions and choices from time to time, in order to help them feel that they are an independent state in their own right.

The Rules of War

From time to time, despite your best efforts, war will break out. In these difficult times, it is important to remember a few ground rules in order to minimise the damage and blood spillage.

Keep Calm: If you wade into the argument all guns blazing, all hell will break loose. Cease fire and retain your cool.

Ignorance is Bliss: Avoid conflict by walking away and taking no notice. Beware of attacks to the back of the knees using sharp implements.

Containment: Place your child into a safe room by himself until peace is restored. Only use this tactic with children over 18 months, and keep 'time out' less than 2 minutes in length.

Undertake Warning Fire: If combat threatens, explain to the enemy why their actions are unacceptable, and help them to understand their situation.

Avoid Further Negotiations: When the tantrum is over, do not mention it again. You could start World War 3.

Avoiding the Battle of Aisle 4

A common battlefield in which the enemy chooses to engage in war is the supermarket. If this occurs, the rules of war are as follows:

Minimise Your Visits: Like an SAS/Marines mission, you must get in and get out of the supermarket as quickly as possible before a tantrum has time to boil over.

Distract the Enemy: Take a toy to occupy the enemy, as well as a snack or two.

Form an Alliance: Request that the enemy helps you with the shopping, retrieving small items and placing them in your trolley.

Vacate Immediately: If you have attempted to calm the enemy yet a tantrum is imminent, leave your shopping with a store employee and vacate the premises.

You are now fully trained and able to enter the war zone. Look after yourself, soldier. I don't want you coming home in a body bag.

That was fun, wasn't it? I hope it made sense.

DEALING WITH YOUR OWN TEMPER

Let's face it: counting to ten doesn't work.

It's all very well and good dealing with your child's temper tantrums, but both you and I know that you are regularly going to be pushed to the edge by a kid who is, basically, being a brat.

When you find yourselves in situations such as these, it's important that you conduct yourself properly. No-one whacks their kid around the legs with a belt any more, and if you fly into a rage all you're doing is setting a bad example. Also, drugs and alcohol are not the answer.

"Now go to your room!" *vomits*

So, how do you keep your cool when confronted with a child who has painted your TV, snapped your favourite DVD in half, and is generally just being a tool?

Before we look at how to control your temper, though, it's worth reiterating why losing your temper doesn't work. Consider the scenario: your child wants to play with a particular toy, but you know that you've both got to go to your parents for tea in five minutes. You politely refuse, and watch as your kid boils over into a mini-strop.

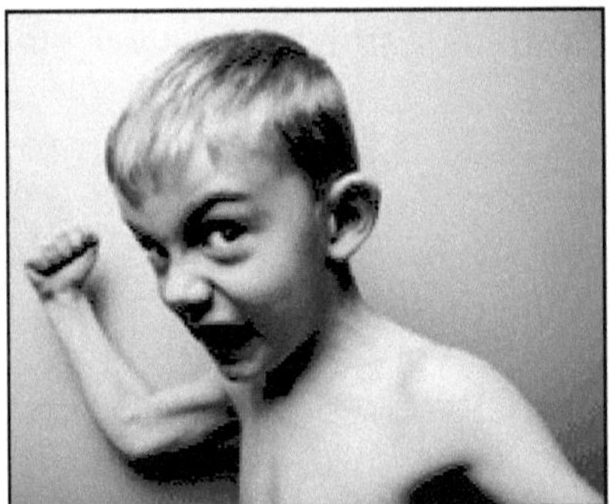

Uh-oh.

You lose your temper, he loses his, and before you know it you're both at each other's throats without having solved the initial problem: in fact, in the heat of the moment, it all goes forgotten and all you end up doing is winding each other up until both of you are on your back, kicking your legs.

So how can you control your frustration when things start going wrong? What do you do when counting to ten doesn't work, or you don't have a wooden spoon handy to chomp down on?

- **Don't take it personally.** One mistake many parents make when their child has a tantrum is viewing it as a reflection on their ability as a mother or father. This is exacerbated when sad single people judge you in the aisle as your child screams away. Ignore them: their judgement doesn't matter. In fact, *they* don't matter. Go give them a kick.

- **Plan ahead.** If you anticipate a tantrum, you can take steps to control the situation before it gets out of hand. For example, you will give your child one warning, and if they don't calm down, you will take them home, or send them to the naughty step. If you plan, you can stay in control, and your stress levels will stay low.

- **Deep breaths.** If you do end up blowing your top, stop as soon as you can and take a few deep breaths. Apologise to your child for losing your temper and give them a hug. Do try to ensure that you follow through with any discipline that you were planning on doling out, though, as your child still needs to learn that their tantrum will not be tolerated.

It is inevitable that you will, on occasion, lose your temper. We're all human, after all. Just make sure that you apologise, calm down, and resist the urge to throw yourself on your back and scream.

KEEP
CALM
AND
DRINK
BEER

GETTING YOUR KID TO STAY IN BED

Restraint straps: outlawed since 1853

Aah. Innit great when your kid's in bed and you can slob out on the settee and watch something pointless and mind-numbing on TV?

But what's that? The creak of floorboards? The patter of chubby little feet across the landing and down the stairs? You look at the door and wait for the inevitable.

Britney Spears?! Well, *that* was unexpected.

OK, so almost never does the pitter-patter of tiny feet across your landing and down your stairs belong to Britney Spears, unfortunately. And don't look at me like that. You know that even when she went through that phase when she was bald, you'd have still had a go.

The door swings open and there is your child, comfort blanket in hand, *knowing* that he's doing the wrong thing but doing it anyway. This appearance is often accompanied by some lame excuse about monsters or something.

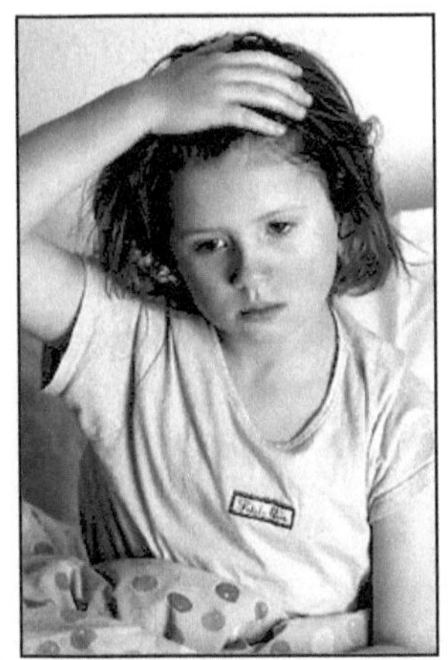
"Britney Spears is under my bed."

"I wish."

So, considering straitjackets, staples, restraint straps, handcuffs, strong rope, superglue and magnets are all pretty much outlawed means of keeping your child in bed, what can you do? Doesn't leave much else, to be honest.

Disclaimer: Please don't tie, staple or glue your child to a bed, or you may find yourself staring at the soap in a prison shower.

The first thing to do is make sure your child **loves his bedroom**. If he likes his room, he's more likely to spend time in it, which is why we men like pubs so much.

Get your child involved in a redecoration of his room – or, if you don't fancy too much work, head down to Ikea and have him pick out a duvet/pillow set that he likes. See if he wants to rearrange the furniture. If he feels more involved in the setup of his bedroom, he's more likely to spend time in it. Or so the theory goes.

Establish an interesting bedtime routine. Come up with a night-time ritual that your child looks forward to, such as reading his favourite book, or having a snack before brushing his teeth. Don't just lob your kid into his bed and expect him to stay there. If you do have a routine established, though, don't repeat it if your child gets up. **Be firm**, and walk him back to his bedroom.

Stay with your child when he goes to bed, but don't hang around for too long, otherwise he might think you'll be there all night. Make sure he knows that you're leaving, by giving him a kiss/high five and saying "See you in the morning".

Make sure your kid **goes to the toilet** before he goes to bed, as the reason for him getting up might simply be that he's busting for the loo.

Before you know it, your child will be staying in bed. And so will you. But then, the next day, you've got to wake up and do it all again. Hurrah!

THE TWO-YEAR DEVELOPMENTAL CHECK

What do you mean, he's not even crawling yet?

We've spoken about developmental checks before in this literary triumph of a book you're holding right now (or reading on some fancy-pants ebook device, you great snob), so we won't spend ages on this one.

Again, disclaimer, if your child doesn't do all of these things, it doesn't mean he's thick. Different kids, different times, you know the drill.

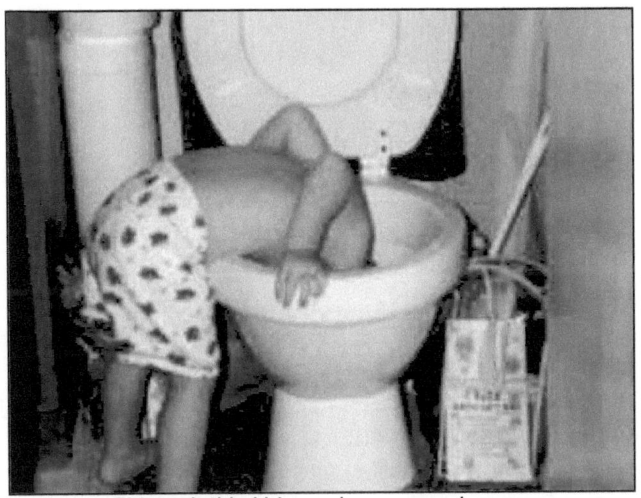

Although this kid may have some issues.

So let's take a look at the kind of things that the health visitor will check for. But first, you'll need to look at the next page.

TWO YEAR DEVELOPMENTAL CHECKLIST

Motor Skills

Can the child:

- ☐ Walk and run without falling
- ☐ Walk upstairs and downstairs
- ☐ Throw a ball without falling over
- ☐ Kick a ball by walking into it
- ☐ Build a tower of 5-6 bricks
- ☐ Turn the single pages of a book

Communication

Can the child:

- ☐ Use a vocabulary of about 50 understandable words
- ☐ Make short sentences of two words
- ☐ Tell you what he needs
- ☐ Carry out simple instructions
- ☐ Recognise simple pictures of everyday objects

Social Skills & Behaviour

Can the child:

- ☐ Play with toys meaningfully and in make believe play
- ☐ Take turns playing with toys when playing alongside another child
- ☐ Drink from a cup and feed self with spoon
- ☐ Demonstrate a high level of curiosity
- ☐ Demonstrate an awareness of when he has wet/soiled himself

With thanks to healthvisitors.com

HOW TO DEAL WITH YOUR CHILD'S FEARS

The Bogeyman is real, and Santa is a paedo

We've all got our fears, even though we're all big butch men who fight dragons and stuff. I, for example, hate steam, and can't walk into the bathroom after my mrs has had a hot shower for a good couple of hours.

I also hate sponges. Even the feel of a sponge makes me want to puke everywhere. I sometimes wake up in a cold sweat after having had a nightmare when I'm being chased by a big sponge. Ironically, I'm so sweaty I need a sponge to mop it all up. Funny how these things happen, isn't it?

I've opened up to you right there, and feel a bit short-changed, as there's no way of you reciprocating the gesture and telling me what you're afraid of. But you know deep down what it is, and one day it will get you.

Argh! Mother in law!

As your child grows, his fears change, and studies have shown that these tend to follow a pattern.

Infants and Young Toddlers

Strangers, mostly. Basically, anyone who isn't you or the mrs.

Eighteen Months

Fears can include animals, sudden noises, doctors and nurses.

Or all at once.

Two Years

The child fears such things as the toilet, the dark, people dressed up (e.g. clowns), and perhaps even Santa Claus.

Two and a Half Years

As your child's imagination develops, it begins to be scared of monsters and other fantasy creatures.

There's not a lot you can do to prevent these fears; it's all a part of growing up. When I was a kid I hated the idea of the Tooth Fairy. It is pretty freaky, when you think about it.

Why does my child have fears?

You've got to remember that these kids haven't been around for very long, and as such have limited life experience. Now and again this results in them putting two and two together and equalling five. For example, they might see water going down the plughole and panic that they will also get drained away; or perhaps get scared by one dog and attribute this fear to all dogs.

Toddlers, like midgets, are also acutely aware that they're a lot smaller than people around them, which can contribute to their fears. They also have the ability to retain a memory: so, whereas your child would have injections as a baby and forget about them the next day, a two year-old might freak out every time you visit the doctor. Even supposedly harmless stories such as Goldilocks and the Three Bears can scare him.

How can I help my child overcome his fear?

The first thing to do is **recognise that his fear is real**. While he might have an overactive imagination, he still believes that what he's conjured up in that double-fist sized brain is an actual thing out to get him.

Try and **find out the source of his fears**, whether it be a DVD he's watched, or a book he's read. It may be simply something he's noticed as you've been out and about.

There are loads of books around that deal with fears in toddlers. If you child is afraid of being drained away with the bathwater, for example, read him a book about a child having fun in the bath. If he's frightened of Father Christmas, **read him a happy story** about a kid who gets lots of presents. If he's worried about the threat of terrorism and the global financial crisis, stop him from reading the Daily Mail.

"The FTSE is falling! WE'RE ALL GONNA DIE!"

Never make fun of your child's fear. It might even be that you've inadvertently projected your own fears on to him: for example, you might pick him up whenever you walk past a dog, or wrench him from the arms of a chubby bearded chap in a red and white outfit who wants nothing more than a cuddle.

Help you child to relax and chill out, and sooner or later his fears will subside. Chances are you've already experienced your biggest fear, and you've survived, haven't you?

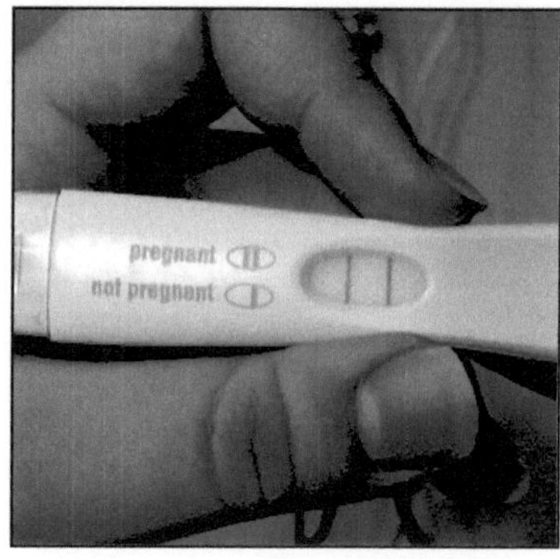

TEN GREAT WAYS TO BOND WITH YOUR KID

Chatting over a pint is not an option

I know I'm preaching to the converted, but it is super-important for any dad to bond with his child. Whether it's wresting with your son, or being mega-protective over your daughter, it's our natural instinct to protect our young. Here are ten simple yet great ways to bond with your child:

1. Give Him a Nickname

Giving your child a nickname is a great way to bond with him or her, especially if it's a funny one (nasty nicknames such as 'buck teeth' or 'four eyes' will have the opposite effect). Call them by this nickname when you're having a great time together to reinforce your bond.

2. Work out a Bedtime Ritual

Reading your child his favourite book at bedtime or playing a game is an ideal way to bond. Once they start being able to read themselves you can have them read back to you, although stick to simple books, because your child will end up hating you if you make him read *War and Peace*.

3. Play with Them

This sounds obvious, but it really is one of the best ways for you to bond with your child. It also gives you a great excuse to act like a kid yourself.

4. Have some One-on-One Time

Every now and then go out somewhere, just you and your child. Although it's obviously important to bond as a family, it's just as critical that you spend some alone time with your little guy or girl to do something fun and boost that father-child bond.

5. Listen to Them

As well as reading him a story and bossing him about, it's important that you listen to what your child has to say. If he recognises that you're genuinely interested in what he has to say then he'll love you all the more.

6. Get in the Kitchen

Look, I know this is a job usually reserved just for women (*ducks thrown knife*) but cooking with your child is a great way to bond. In this instance, 'cooking with your child' means alongside your child, not actually using your child as an ingredient.

7. Sing in the Car

Car journeys can be a stressful time, especially when your child is booting the back of your chair. Instead of getting stressed and glaring in the rear-view mirror, whack a CD on that you both enjoy and have a jolly good sing-along. Even if it is Susan Boyle.

8. Eat Together

Sit down with your kid at the table to eat, instead of balancing a plate on your knees while CBeebies jingles away in the background. Use this time to talk and chat to your child, and make them laugh.

9. Create a Scrapbook

Put a scrapbook together that is full of photos of you and your child. Allow your kid to decorate each page. It'll get super-messy, but you'll have bags of fun.

10. Say "I love you"

I know, I know, it's mega-soppy – but it's true. Tell your child every day that you love them; and, if you're lucky, they might even say it back.

Don't do this when standing under a helicopter.

MILESTONES

If you rearrange the letters in the word 'milestones' you get the name 'Simon Steel', which would be a great pseudonym for a wrester, or 'Most Senile', which is what you'll be once your child finally leaves home.

You also get 'Eel Snit Oms', which makes little sense.

13 Months

- Uses two words skilfully, for example 'hello' and 'bye'
- Bends over to pick up an object
- Stands without help

14 Months

- Finger feeds
- Imitates others

15 Months

- Plays with a ball
- Five-word vocabulary
- Can walk backwards

16 Months

- Turns the pages of a book
- Has temper tantrums
- Becomes attached to a soft toy or other comforting object

17 Months

- Has a handful of words in his vocabulary
- Likes riding toys

18 Months

- Scribbles well
- Pedals when put on a tricycle

19 Months

- Can use a spoon and fork
- Can run
- Can throw a ball underarm

20 Months

- Can take off own clothes without help
- Throws away rubbish into a bin

21 Months

- Can walk up steps
- Can follow simple instructions

22 Months

- Can kick a ball forward
- Follows instructions with two steps (eg. Pick up your doll and bring it to me)
- Imitates others' behaviour

23 Months

- Can make a tower from 4-6 bricks
- Can name simple pictures
- Has a vocabulary of 50 words

24 Months

- Can name at least six body parts
- Can construct short sentences

25-26 Months

- Can name several body parts

27-28 Months

- Speaks clearly most of the time
- Puts on clothes

- Jumps off the ground

29-30 Months

- Brushes teeth with help
- Washes and dries hands

31-32 Months

- Can throw a ball overarm

33-34 Months

- Can name one or more colours
- Carries on a conversation of two or three sentences

35-36 Months

- Can describe how two objects are used
- Uses four to five words in a sentence
- Can name two actions, such as skipping or jumping

Information from babycentre.co.uk

SECTION THREE

PRESCHOOL

(3-4 years)

Crumbs, he's growing up fast. Soon he'll be a teenager, with a face full of grease and acne, emitting grunts of disgust as the waistband of his jeans cling awkwardly to the underside of his buttocks in some kind of ridiculous fashion statement. Such a magical time.

At this stage in your child's life, he is probably going to nursery or preschool. This presents another great big batch of challenges that you will probably have to deal with, as if changing millions of nappies and being kicked in the face countless times isn't paying your dues enough.

Believe it or not, though, this is the time when your child begins to become less dependent upon you as a father, and begins to establish his own independence as well as mastering his socialising skills. Don't celebrate too soon, though. It won't be long until he's begging you for money.

Anyway, let's crack on. It's page 148, for crying out loud. You must be incredibly bored of me by now.

NIGHT TERRORS

What your mrs gets when she imagines you naked

They started out of the blue: about an hour after he went to sleep, our 3 year-old son would start crying and screaming, sometimes shaking with fear. When we would comfort him, he would look at us with utter fear in his eyes and cling onto our arms. This would last for about ten minutes, and then he would simply lie down and fall back to sleep as if nothing had happened.

"Well *that* was weird..."

I did what every concerned parent would do in a situation like this: I Googled the heck out of it. And it seems we're not alone.

Around 15% of children experience night terrors, or *pavor nocturmus*, if you want to use the medical term, you nerd: a parasomnia disorder characterised by a temporary inability to regain full consciousness combined with terror attacks.

Night terror can also occur in adults, although they are much less common, and often based on trauma, like imagining yourself running naked on a treadmill in front of a mirror.

Your child, if he or she suffers from night terrors, has no recollection of the event in the morning, which is less than can be said you or I.

That's why, in the morning, your kid is all like:

And you're all like:

As with all these things, knowing more about this disorder can help you understand how to prevent them from occurring. Which is why I'm here. For you. You're welcome.

Night terrors. Symptoms. Now.

Rude.

Night terrors are most common in children aged two to six, although adults can also suffer from parasomnia (also a good name for a band). They can carry on for weeks and then suddenly disappear, and are characterised by a period of upset and terror for the child, who may sit upright and have his or her eyes open. They could also display 'fight or flight' bodily reactions, such as sweating, quick breathing and an increased heart rate.

Night terrors usually begin about 15 minutes to one hour after the child falls asleep, and last for 10-20 minutes, during which the child may appear confused and inconsolable. Although the child seems awake, he is still unconscious, and may not recognise you.

What causes night terrors?

Night terrorists.

The good news is that your child hasn't been possessed by demons. Night terrors are often

triggered by physical or emotional stress, such as beginning at school or moving house. The child may also have been stimulated mentally before sleep – for example, they have read a book about monsters and dragons, which could trigger a terror attack. If you read him that book, then shame on you.

The most common cause for night terrors is sleep deprivation. The average three year-old needs around 11 or 12 hours of sleep per night, and so if your child is getting less you may wish to put them to bed slightly earlier.

How can I prevent night terrors?

Stress is one of the biggest night terror triggers, so make sure your child has a relaxing evening. Give him time to chill out before bed: give him a warm bath, play calm music and read him a soothing book. You can also give him foods that help to induce sleep: a glass of milk, apple slices with peanut butter, or a raisin and oatmeal biscuit.

Avoid Red Bull.

Make sure the room is not too hot, as this can also be a factor in triggering an episode. You may also wish to use herbal remedies to help him relax, such as chamomile capsules, or perhaps the scent of lavender.

If your child does have a night terror attack, keep calm and reflect this by using soothing tones. Reassure and cuddle him, to prevent him from hurting himself or others. Some parents find that gently awakening their child just before they go to bed themselves helps to prevent night terrors; similarly, if your child has attacks at roughly the same time every night, awaken him 15 minutes before the episode usually begins.

In many cases, these methods will help prevent night terror attacks. In a minority of cases a trip to the doctor may be required to see if there are any underlying causes for the episodes. But don't worry: eventually, you will get a full night's sleep. Eventually.

HOW TO CHOOSE A DECENT PRESCHOOL

Preferably one without any room behind the bike sheds

The temptation, when it comes to choosing a preschool, is to get so carried away with the notion that your child might be off your hands for a few hours a day that you just lob him into the nearest one. And I mean physically lob. Over the fence, and whatnot.

Just to confirm: I got this photo off the Internet.
I didn't grab an actual child and hook him on a fence just to prove a point.

However, the vast majority of parents are keen for their child to have a good education, and preschool lays the foundations for success later on in your child's academic life, i.e. *not* going to Grange Hill.

Choosing the right preschool, then, can be a tricky and drawn-out process, and because we men don't like tricky and drawn-out processes, I'm going to simplify it.

When can my kid go to preschool?

Most preschools or nurseries take children on from two years and nine months old; but, if you feel your child is ready before this stage, have a word with the staff.

When should we start looking?

Start looking a few months before your child is due to start. This gives you lots of time to prepare and procrastinate.

What kind of things should I look out for?

You can analyse the heck out of each preschool you visit to try and work out whether it's the right one for your child; but it really boils down to a few important things.

A Good Reputation

Ask around your newly-acquired parent friends about preschools in the area. They'll usually direct you to the ones they consider to be the best. If you keep hearing the same name coming up time after time, then you've got yourself a good sign.

The best thing to do is to go and see the school for yourself, and trust your instincts. A good preschool will allow you to drop by unannounced, and maybe even invite your child to a 'taster' session in order to mingle with the children and activities (actually tasting the children is frowned upon).

On the subject of tasting, though, find out about the school's policy on nutrition. If they're providing food, what do they give the kids to eat? If you're packing a lunchbox, is there anything you're not allowed to give to your child while he's in school, such as sweets?

When you're there, look at the children and staff. If you see kids moping about with nothing to do, and disinterested teachers, you can safely assume that they're not having much fun. Then, after your keen assumption, you should grab your child and run like heck.

Decent Policies

A good, well-organised preschool will have written and detailed policies about everything to do with the school, from handling emergencies to the food given to the kids. This shows that they take their responsibilities seriously, and are looking out for the welfare of both your child and the other pupils.

A Good Curriculum

Any preschool worth its salt will have a strong syllabus and curriculum to make sure that the kids have a good mix of things to do throughout the day, such as quiet time, team activities, crafts, and so on.

This curriculum should be regularly updated and juggled around a bit to make sure the children don't fall into a routine and become bored, as well as being appropriate to the age of children attending the school (no algebra, for example).

Qualified Staff

A good preschool employs experienced and qualified staff, who are enthusiastic about their role in teaching your child. They should be trained in basic first aid as well as having great interpersonal skills to get the best out of your son or daughter.

Make sure the teacher:pupil ratio is enough to ensure that each child has regular interaction with a member of staff, and is not left simply to do his own thing.

A Clean Environment

If the school smells like dead animals, has plaster peeling off the walls, and you've had to step over three mounds of cat poo in the hallway, it's not for you. A decent school takes pride in its facilities, and recognises the need for good hygiene.

Take a good look around when visiting a potential preschool, and note whether toys are in a good condition, if play equipment is safe, and whether or not there are fire extinguishers around.

A good preschool should also have an outside area for children to play in, boosting their physical and social skills.

Do Your Homework

In the United Kingdom of Great Britain and Northern Ireland, we have the benefit of those guys at Ofsted/Deni/HMIe, who go around preschools and mark them on all of the things we've just spoken about. Get onto the Internet, find the right website and do a search for your preferred school. You should be able to read the latest report, which will give you a great idea of just how good the school is.

Unfortunately, it doesn't tell you whether any of the teachers are hot.

SETTLING YOUR CHILD INTO PRESCHOOL

Or, how to make sure you don't have to pick them up after an hour

You know how you feel when you start your first day in a new job? You're a bit nervous, you don't know anyone, people keep looking at you funny, and you panic all the time about whether your fly is open?

Now imagine that, but with your new colleagues screaming, shouting, throwing things and generally making a massive mess. That's what the first day of preschool is like for your child.

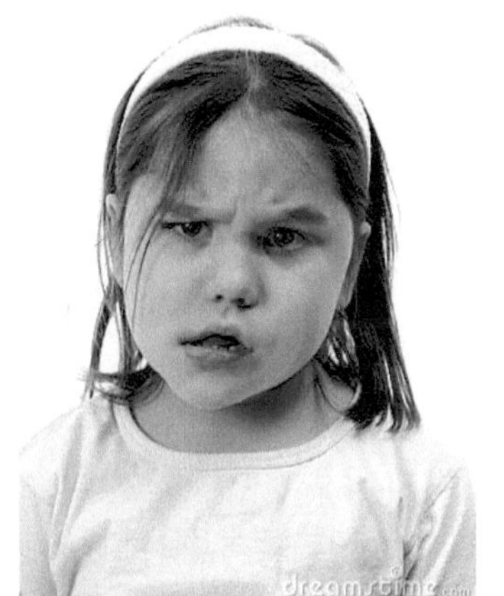

"What the hell have I walked into?!"

A new school can be pretty overwhelming, and your child may become very shy and introvert. Fortunately, there are a number of things you can do to stop them from burying their face in your crotch and clinging on to your thighs.

the ben wakeling preschool
for preschool age kids

daily timetable

quiet time

quiet time

quiet time

home time

Before Starting Preschool

Preparing your child for a life in school is vitally important in ensuring they settle in well. Suddenly picking them up and plonking them in the middle of a crowded room full of screaming people is akin to someone throwing us into the sharp end of a firefight in Iraq.

Talk to your child about preschool, but obviously do it in a cheerful way. Don't talk in ominous, scary tones or anything. Instead, show excitement about all the fun he'll have, or all the new friends he'll make.

If the school are happy for you to do so, **tour the school with your kid**. As well as providing you with an opportunity to get last-minute questions answered, it will help your son or daughter become familiar with new surroundings.

Have a **get-together with other families** whose kids will be attending the same school. This means that your child will see some familiar faces on the first day and feel more at ease.

On the First Day

Make sure that you **go with your child** on the first day, as opposed to shoving them out the car door as you cruise by. You can meet their teachers and be an initial point of security for them.

Pack a lunchbox with treats to brighten their day and help them feel happier. These could be in the form of chocolates, or perhaps little notes, although your child probably can't read at this point, so go with the chocolates thing.

Ongoing Support

If your child has made a few close friends, make sure you **meet up regularly** with their families so that their friendships can strengthen. Many kids will 'graduate' to the same first and middle schools from preschool, and so your child could have made a couple of friends for life.

"I graduated in burping the alphabet and soiling myself!"

You can also enrol your child in any **extra-curricular activities** that the preschool may offer, in order to help him socialise more, or nurture a growing talent or skill.

Make sure you **talk to him** about his day, what he's been doing, and so on. Keep an eye out for any changes in behaviour which could indicate that he's not having a great time.

Most of all, you should **give it time**. Chances are your child is not going to stroll into school and instantly pick up friends, so if he seems a little lonely for the first few days or weeks then give him support and don't panic. If you are concerned, then **talk to the teachers** to find out how he's getting on and if he seems upset while he's at school. There could be a reason for it if he does, which leads us on nicely to the next chapter. I'm awesome like that.

HOW TO DEAL WITH PRESCHOOL BULLIES

Apparently, flying knee kicks are illegal

Getting home from work is my favourite time of the day. Both kids go mental like they've just won the lottery or something, I get nice hugs, result.

There has been one instance, though, when I got home and things were different. Noah started laughing and kicking his legs as per usual; but Isaac stood with his back to me, watching CBeebies.

"Isaac," I call, "Daddy's home!"

He turns, and I instantly notice a large scratch down his left cheek, about an inch or two long.

Eyes widen. "What happened?"

My wife appears at the kitchen door and beckons me over. It turns out that some kid in Isaac's class at preschool has been picking on him: calling him names, and whatnot. From what she can gather, it's been going on for a while. Today it progressed into a physical attack, with the bully clawing his nails down Isaac's face. The teachers didn't know what had happened, because Isaac was too scared to tell them the truth. It was only when he was at home that he opened up to his mum.

I start seething, and approach Isaac. I lift him up so he's standing on the dining room table, his eyes level with mine.

"What happened to your cheek?" I ask, in my softest voice, even though my jaw seems to be in a permanent state of clench.

"Someone scratched me." He looks at me, big eyes all innocent. He tells me the bully's name.

"Is he mean to lots of boys and girls?"

"No. Just me."

I give him a big hug and put him down onto the carpet. By now, my blood is boiling. I mean, *literally* boiling. I can hear it bubbling in my veins.

Take this and multiply it by infinity.

Now, don't get me wrong: I would never hit a child. But, right then, all I wanted to do was flying knee kick the bully in the face, roundhouse him in the knees and then scratch *his* face with a rusty spoon. Livid, I was, and to be honest I'd never known anger like it. I wasn't throwing furniture around or anything; just stood in the lounge, fists clenched, snarling like some kind of caged lion.

I couldn't help but imagine the whole scene: Isaac's expression when this kid called him names, the pain he must have been in when he was scratched. By now, my anger crosshairs had shifted to this child's parents. I wanted to put a brick through their window and torch their car. (I didn't, obv.)

As moving as your story is, I'm kinda bored. Get to the point.

Fine. Both you and I need to know what to do to resolve the situation when rearranging a 4 year-old's face is out of the question. But first, you need to work out whether or not your child is being bullied in the first place.

Identifying whether or not your child is being bullied in the first place

There are a number of tell-tale signs that your child might be being picked on. These include:

- Being suddenly afraid to go to preschool;
- Complaining of illness for no reason;
- Being clingy or whingy;
- Comes home with unexplained injuries;
- Being withdrawn;
- Avoids eye contact when you talk about school;
- Complaining about one particular person doing mean things to them.

The last one on that list is a kind of obvious indication that something is up.

What to do when Your Child is Bullied

Firstly, you need to **communicate with your child**. Let him or her know that you are here to listen to their fears, and that you will make everything better. There are even a couple of books on the market that deal specifically with this topic, and reading a few of these might bring your child out of his shell.

Speaking to the teacher is also a good idea – emphasis on 'speaking'. You're not going to achieve anything if you burst open the teacher's door with a single kick, and demand that something be done. Remember that they can't be everywhere all the time, so it is inevitable that now and again a bit of bullying may go unnoticed. Tell them what has happened, and rest assured they will keep a close eye on the situation and make sure it doesn't happen again. The teachers could even set up a meeting between you and the bully's parents if you so wish – just be prepared that they may deny that their little cherub could *ever* do such terrible things...

Do not teach your child kung-fu, or how to be a ninja. Instead, **give him the confidence to stand up to the bully** next time it happens by refusing to be intimidated and informing a teacher. You could even carry out a short role-playing scenario with your child so they know both how to deal with a bully in the future, and how to avoid situations where they may be bullied – for example, if they become detached from their group of friends.

Sometimes, the bullying becomes so bad that you are forced to move classes or even schools. **Talk to as many professionals as you can** before you make this move, as it could be detrimental to your child's self-esteem to take them away from their friends and into a totally new environment. This should be a last resort, though.

There is one more thing you can do, which might not go down well at first. **Invite the bully over to**

play with your child. You may find that, outside school, the bully and your kid actually play really well together; you never know. But it is possible that the worst of enemies could become the best of friends.

It's a funny thing, the natural instinct for a parent to protect his or her young. We ain't nothin' but mammals, as the Bloodhound Gang once sang, although in an entirely different context.

Approach a bear cub, and his mum will blunder over and take your face off with one swipe. Try to nick a bird's egg, and prepare to get your eyes clawed out by a furious pigeon. Scratch my son, and I'll punt you through the nearest window. Either that, or I'll have to put up with telling the teacher.

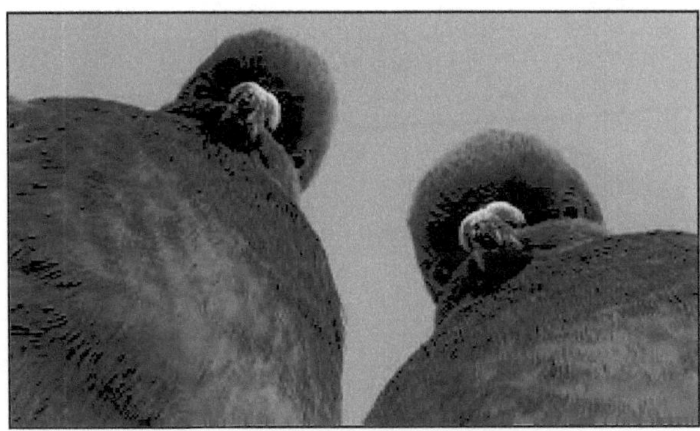

Don't mess with the pigeons.
They know where you've parked.

FOOD AND NUTRITION

McDonalds and KFC don't really count

I have a thing about old women evilling me as they shuffle past just because I'm tucking into a Big Mac and large fries. I'd understand if I was eating over 100% of my Recommended Daily Allowance of fat and crud, but I'm not. So back off, grandma.

You don't need me to tell you, though, that you should feed your kid the right diet, and that plying them with daily Bargain Buckets will probably end up making them look like this.

Or this.

Also, don't let them smoke.

That's not to say the odd fast food meal is some kind of super-sin. We're all allowed one day off from eating healthily, right? Although in my case, it's seven days off a week. And now I have three chins.

Anyway, back to the point. It's good to encourage your kid to eat good food. But, guess what? Preschoolers are mega-picky about what they eat. This presents us with our first problem.

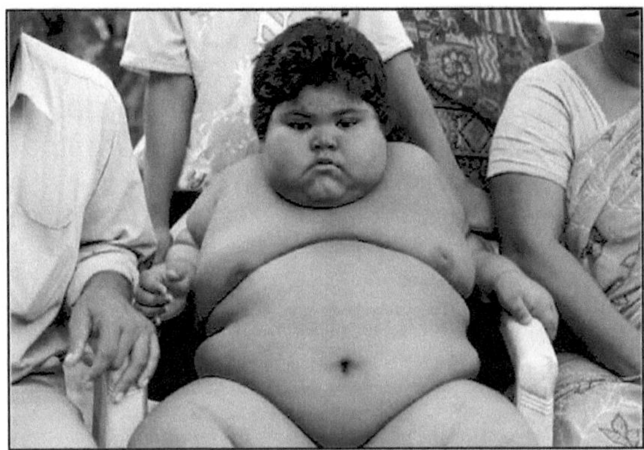

OK, enough of the fat kids.

How can I encourage my child to eat?

Preschoolers are notoriously choosy about what they do and do not eat. You will be aware of this if you've ever had to shovel a piece of broccoli down the throat of your three year-old child.

The trick is to **keep calm**, and not make a big deal of it. If you draw attention to it, or try and force him to eat, he's just going to become even unhappier.

Instead of putting all your effort into crowbaring your child's mouth open, try to **make mealtimes a fun experience**. Get your child involved in cooking the meal, if possible; he is a lot more likely to eat something he's played an active part in.

Always provide both a sweet and savoury course, so your kid has plenty of opportunity to experience different tastes and get as many nutrients down him as he can.

Try to **avoid making him a separate meal**, but instead give him a smaller portion of what you're having. This will prevent you from getting into the rut of just giving him fishfingers and smiley faces every mealtime.

Finally, really ham (no pun intended, but awesome nonetheless) it up when you're eating food. Give it all "Mmm, this is so tasty" and you'll soon find your kid wants to know what all the fuss is about.

What are the important nutrients for a preschooler?

As important as it is that your child gets a well-rounded diet, you should aim to make sure that he regularly receives certain vitamins and minerals, to make sure he grows up to be a BIG STRONG BOY.

Calcium

You've seen the adverts for fromage frais when they bang on about all the calcium making your bones and teeth strong. Turns out, they're true.

Make sure your child receives three servings of calcium-rich food each day, such as a glass of milk or a small yoghurt. Other sources of calcium include cheese, fortified orange juice, cereals and sesame seeds.

Folate

Not only did your child need Folic Acid when your mrs was necking it during pregnancy, but he also could do with it now, for healthy growth.

These can be found in fortified cereals, bread, leafy veg and pulses.

Iron

While iron-deficiency anaemia is more common in primary school kids, it can affect preschoolers as well. Iron is essential for keeping red blood cells working correctly and helping the transportation of blood around the body.

Therefore, make sure your child regularly scoffs iron-rich foods such as red meat, liver, cereals, beans and pulses.

Although good luck with giving him liver.

Fats and Sugar

Fats and sugar?! But we spend most of our lives being told by lispy chefs that too much fat and sugar is WRONG and will make our child into the next human whale!

My word, he's ripe for milking.

The fact is that fats and sugars are vital for the body to continue working properly, and are only dangerous when consumed in large amounts. You don't really need me to tell you which foods have sugar and fat in them. It'd be easier for me to tell you the foods which *don't*.

What should he drink?

Be careful with sugar-free or diet fizzy drinks as well; although they might have fewer calories or ladles of sugar, the acidity can still make a hefty contribution towards tooth decay.

Also, while I'm lecturing you, try and give your preschooler drinks in a cup or beaker – bottles or cups with a lid that you suck from prolongs exposure to harmful sugars in the drink.

handy alternatives to sweets

COMMON ILLNESSES AMONGST PRESCHOOLERS

Mmmmm, nits.

Now that your child is an 'orrible snotty preschooler, he's going to be in close contact with lots of other 'orrible snotty preschoolers on a daily basis, which means his chances of catching an illness are pretty much certain. In fact, I'm so certain that your kid will - at some point - get some kind of contagious bug from his classmates that I'm willing to place a wager.

Send my winnings to Buckingham Palace.
I'll pick 'em up next time I stop by to see Lizzy.

There are some illnesses or conditions that are highly common amongst preschoolers for this very reason. I figured that if I tell you about them you'll know what to do **when** it happens. Yes, when. I'm waiting for my cash.

In no particular order, certainly not alphabetical 'cos I can't be bothered:

Chickenpox

Yes, it is all one word.

I didn't know this until I became a dad, but some parents are so keen for their child to get chickenpox that they organise special 'chickenpox parties' when someone in the school comes down with the illness, just so their kid will catch it. I've never been to one of these parties, but I envisage it being one very itchy scabby child assuming the foetal position in the middle of the room while the other kids take turns to come up and lick his face. Maybe.

Chickenpox is, probably the number one illness that most parents worry about during preschool age.

What are the symptoms?

The most obvious symptom of chickenpox is a **red rash that covers the body**. Some people only have a few spots, some have them *everywhere*. It's usually found behind the ears, on the face and scalp, under the arms or on the chest and stomach.

The rash starts as itchy red spots, turning into mega-itchy blisters after about 12-14 hours. These crust over after 1-4 days, eventually disappearing in a couple of weeks.

Symptoms can also include **nausea**, **fever** and **loss of appetite**. These symptoms are also commonly associated with marriage.

How can I cure it?

There is no cure.

There are, however, things you can do to help ease the symptoms.

Painkillers such as paracetamol or ibuprofen will help to lower a high temperature, but consult your GP if your child has asthma before giving him ibuprofen.

Do not give your child aspirin. Studies have proven a link between treating chickenpox with aspirin and a potentially fatal condition known as Reye's syndrome, which can cause brain and liver damage.

Make sure your child has **plenty of fluids**, to avoid dehydration. If your kid has a sore mouth, which can happen in severe cases, a sugar-free ice lolly will do the trick. **Avoid salty foods**, as this can irritate ulcers inside the mouth.

If your child is scratching excessively, consider **putting socks on his hands**. As well as breaking the skin and drawing blood, intense scratching can cause infection.

Calamine lotion is great for soothing itchy blisters, and is safe to use. Your GP may prescribe **chlorphenamine**, which also relieves itching.

Why the hell is it called chickenpox? My kid ain't no chicken.

There are a number of theories as to the origin of the name 'chickenpox':

- The blisters on the skin look as though your child has been pecked by a number of chickens, or just one enthusiastic chicken;
- The disease was named after chick peas, due to the similarity in size of the blisters;
- The term is a corruption of the Old English word 'giccin', which means 'itching'.

So now you know.

Nits

One day, you'll notice your child scratching his head, and you'll get that horrible feeling in your stomach. Reluctantly, you'll beckon him over and pull apart strands of his hair with tentative fingers. And then you come face to face with THIS.

Not actual size, thankfully.

The term 'nits' actually only refers to the eggs of the head lice, which are laid along strands of hair in little clumps. But you don't care about that. All you want to do is nuke the little gits.

Tell me more about head lice, please.

Umm…OK, if you *really* want to know.

Head lice can't jump. Let's get that myth straightened out, for starters. You're thinking of fleas, who most definitely *can* jump.

Head lice find their way into your child's hair by crawling onto it from another child's hair. They have no preference as to whether your kid's hair is clean or dirty (Boom! Another myth busted). They're just happy to have found a home.

The female head louse will lay her eggs at the base of the strand of hair, where they will be kept warm by the scalp and hatch after about a week, leaving the little eggshells in place. As the hair grows, these eggshells are carried along, and become more noticeable as they're further away from the murky depths of your child's scalp.

These cute little lice will get their food by biting your child's scalp and getting a good ol' bellyful of blood. After 6-10 days, they reach their fully-grown length of 3mm, and either live out their days lurking in your daughter's pigtails or trek on over to another child's head. And then, the cycle begins again.

Now my head is itchy.

Mine too.

How can I get rid of head lice?

There are a number of methods available to zap head lice, although none of them will prevent the little blighters from returning, should your dearest child decide to bump heads with a nit-infested classmate.

Wet combing is one of the cheapest ways to remove head lice, and involves thoroughly combing the hair with a fine nit comb, with spacing between teeth of less than 0.3mm.

Unlike Mick Jagger's daughter.

Nit combs range from the standard to electric combs, which zap the lice on contact. All ranges of comb, though, require meticulous and painstaking combing from root to tip, being sure to wash the comb in a bowl of warm water and disinfectant between runs. The hair should have just been washed and cleaned, with plenty of conditioner so the little ratbags can't cling on for dear life.

"Must...hold...on..."

Using **medicated shampoos, lotions and sprays** is another way of ridding your kid's hair of the dreaded lice. It's tricky, however, to find one that is 100% effective, unless you dunk your child's head into a bowl of sulphuric acid or set his hair on fire, which is completely not a recommended course of action.

Follow the instructions on the bottle, and repeat after seven days. Make sure you get a product that kills the eggs as well as the lice, otherwise they'll simply come back after a few days.

Hopefully, your child will be one of the lucky ones and avoid head lice altogether. In the meantime, here's what the head lice version of *The Simpsons* looks like.

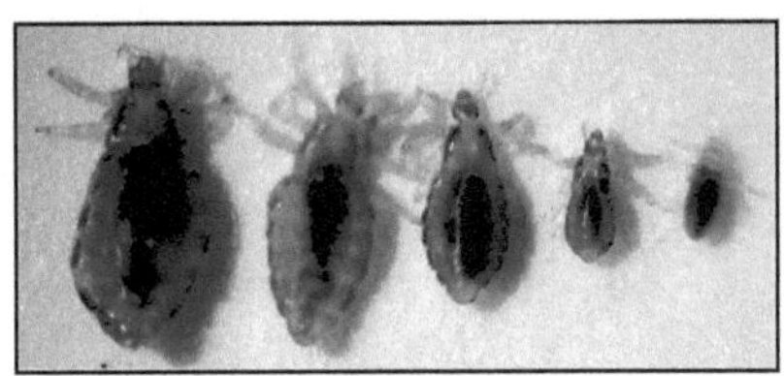

Ringworm

Eww. Why can't these illnesses have nice names, like 'Pink Pony', or 'Feather Dust'. "My kid's got a bad case of feather dust."

As has Elton John.

The good news is that ringworm has absolutely nothing to do with worms. It's actually a general term used to describe a skin condition caused by a group of fungi called dermatophytes. It is highly contagious, passed from child to child through skin contact and sharing objects such as towels or sheets.

What are the symptoms?

Symptoms include **small patches of scaly skin**, commonly on the scalp, which causes itchiness. Some children may also experience **patchy hair loss, sores** and a **rash**.

These sores can occur on the scalp, body or groin, and ringworm is the main culprit behind athlete's foot. This condition, characterised by a rash between the toes, can spread to becoming a full-blown fungal nail infection.

Gross. Treatment?

Scalp ringworm will usually be treated via **oral antifungal medicine**, such a terbinafine or griseofulvin, which sound like character names from the Lord of the Rings.

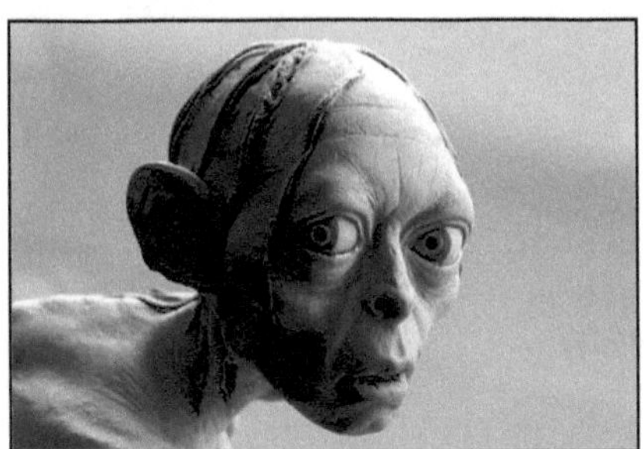

"Alright. I'm Terbinafine. And you are…?"

These tablets do, however, have side effects, including nausea, diarrhoea, indigestion and skin rashes, which are also common by-products of marriage. Have I already used that joke? Sorry.

Many cases of body ringworm, including groin infections, can be treated using **antifungal cream**, available over the counter from your local pharmacy. This is applied daily for two weeks to clear up the infection.

This is a regular worm. Nothing to do with ringworm.

Mumps

Want to look like a python swallowing a goat? Then get mumps.

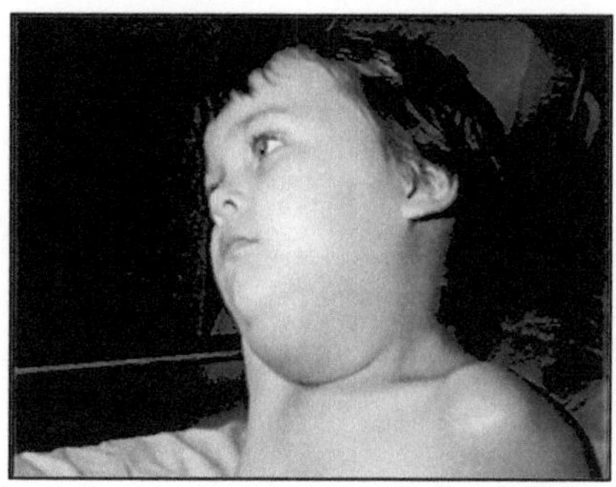

Also, uncanny.

I had mumps once: it was flippin' horrible. The only good thing about it is it's one of those 'if you've had it once you can't usually get it again' illnesses.

What are the symptoms?

I just showed you. Can you not see those pictures?

Apart from a **swelling of the parotid glands**, located on one or both sides of the face, other symptoms include **headache, joint pain, fever** and **loss of appetite**, which is hardly surprising.

You're going to tell me there's no cure, aren't you.

Yeah, sorry. Mumps is a viral infection, which means that there are no medicines on the market at the moment to directly treat it. You can only try, as with other conditions, to ease the symptoms.

Plenty of rest is a good idea, as with a neck the width of your hips you're not going to feel much like partying. **Painkillers** will reduce temperature and help with swelling, but again – **do not use aspirin.** As a general rule, avoid giving children aged 16 or under aspirin at all for pain relief.

Drink plenty of fluids, but avoid things like fruit juice. These stimulate the production of saliva, which can cause more pain. Water is the safest option. **Eating soup and other blended foods** is also a good idea. Finally, **applying a cold compress** to the swelling will help to reduce the pain.

Rubella (German Measles)

What's worse than getting measles? Getting German measles.

Pillock.

Obviously, German measles is not as a direct result of Nazism, but so called because it was German boffins who figured out that it is caused by a different virus than normal measles. But it's fun to blame them nonetheless.

Symptome, bitte.

Symptoms of rubella include **a slightly raised temperature, conjunctivitis** and **a sore throat**. Basically, just generally feeling unwell. To be honest, there's not much point talking about rubella, as it has been pretty much wiped out in the UK thanks to immunisation.

Tell me how to treat it anyway, for completeness more than anything.

The usual, to be honest: **painkillers, fluids** and **bedrest**. I'm not going to talk about it any more, for the same reason I'm not going to talk about leprosy.

These are just a few of the illnesses that preschool kids often get. I could list more, but then this would turn into some kind of medical text book, which would be both pointless and pretty boring.

Talking of which...

HOW TO GET YOUR KID TO TAKE HIS MEDICINE

Otherwise, you end up with a puddle of antibiotics and sick on your shoes.

A while ago, Isaac had tonsillitis, and was prescribed antibiotics. This is what happened when we tried to give them to him.

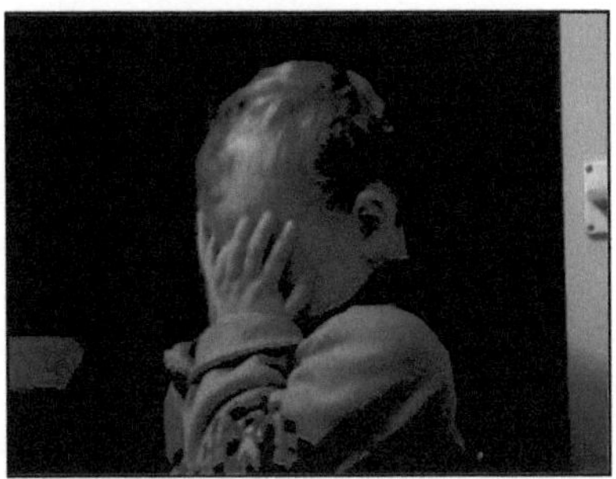

When I finally managed to pry his hands away from his face and squirt the familiar yellow medicine into his clamped mouth using a syringe, he promptly yakked all over himself, me and most of the furniture. This is obviously most unhelpful.

Many parents can empathise; and, short of strapping your kid up in a straitjacket and sitting on him, you might find it a tad tricky to give him something which will ultimately help him.

Here, then, are some great and simple ways to essentially fool your child into taking his medication.

Try to get **liquid medicine** instead of tablets, as this will (should) be easier for him to take. The medicine may be available in a range of flavours, so make sure you ask your GP or pharmacist.

Make up a story to help your child take his medicine. When I was little, my dad told me that the medicine I was refusing had lots of little soldiers in it, who would fight against the nasty bugs in my body. For some reason, I found this appealing, and took the medicine. It was only recently that I realised these were ALL LIES.

A good indication of my face upon said realisation.

Mix the medicine with something sweet such as honey, especially if the medicine is in tablet form. Check with your GP before you do this, though, as some medication does not dissolve easily.

Use a syringe to administer the medicine. It didn't work for me, but hopefully you'll have better luck. Don't do what I did and squirt the medicine straight down his throat, otherwise it'll come right back at you. Aim for the cheek.

Try to **involve your child** as you give him your medicine. He can choose the spoon, perhaps, or take it in little sips.

If all else fails, **bribe your child with sweets.** It's not good for their teeth, but it'll get the darn stuff down them.

SORTING OUT BEHAVIOURAL PROBLEMS

Newsflash: your child isn't a little angel.

You might have visions of your child being wonderful, constantly obedient, always willing, friendly with other kids, kind and helpful. If you do have these visions, you need a right good backhand slap.

Maybe from Ronald McDonald himself.

Your child is his own person, and even though you do your very best to raise him well, there will be times and phases where he'll be a right pillock. These are just some of the wonderful behavioural traits that your little sweetness will demonstrate at this point in his life, as he becomes more independent and forms his own character.

Aggression

Whether through fear, tiredness or frustration, there will be times when your child lashes out at another kid, or even at you. Once he or she grows up and learns to use words to achieve what they want instead of fists, then the aggression should cease.

Unless, of course, your child turns out to be Steven Seagal.

Argh! He's going to roundhouse me! What do I do?

The first thing to do is **make him know he's doing wrong.** Put him on the naughty step, take him away from the situation...whatever works for you and him. **Resist the urge to shout** - this just teaches him that anger is acceptable. Set a good example, defuse the situation, and your child should connect action with consequence. **Repeat this plan** every time the situation arises.

Once your child has chilled out, **discuss what happened** with him. Ask why he became aggressive, and that it is unacceptable to hit, bite, kick or karate chop anyone else.

If your child's aggression breaks something, **make sure he helps to fix it**. This will instil a sense of responsibility in him, and help him to recognise that he has a part to play in resolving the situation.

Reward him when he is good, such as when he asks politely or waits his turn. Just don't reward him with kickboxing lessons, as this pretty much negates everything you've taught him.

Defiance

"No..." you say, in your best low stern dad-voice. Your child looks at you. He's about to empty the contents of the fruit bowl all over the floor.

"No...!" Sterner this time, and perhaps a little bit lower.

He does it anyway. Hoorah.

Defiance is another by-product of growing up: your child is learning how to control his impulses and pushing the boundaries of what he can get away with.

How do I prevent this?

Kids hate to be told they can't have fun, even when their idea of 'fun' is setting fire to the cat. His perception that you are ruining a good time for him will naturally result in a bit of a strop, and Milly ending up with half a tail.

The first step is to **congratulate good behaviour**. If he does something good, no matter how simple, then praise him. Be careful, though, not to do this too much, or it could lose its appeal and impact.

Give him an opportunity to make his own decisions. Being in charge of little tasks, such as the clothes he's going to wear, or which food he would like to eat, will help to prevent defiance and boost confidence.

Make sure that you **warn him in advance** if you will be curtailing his fun: for example, let him know that it will be time for dinner in a few minutes, or that he's going to have to leave his friend's house and come home. This will prepare him for the inevitable, and he should react in a much less defiant fashion.

Ignoring You

This is the one that winds me up the most. I ask Isaac to do something, but get no response. I ask again: no response. I freak out and start crying. No response.

A nervous breakdown follows.

The thing is, preschoolers have little concept of time. They couldn't give a stuff if you're in a hurry; hell, they don't even know what being in a hurry feels like. They don't realise that their safety might be in imminent danger, they just want to get a closer look at the cat licking itself on the other side of the road.

I've told him 'No' a thousand times, but he's still ignoring me. What do?

Try not to say no. Chances are, he's heard it so many times before that the word has lost all meaning. Instead, try to rephrase your statement. If your child is kicking a football around the lounge, just say "You might break something in here. Why don't we go outside?" He gets to still have fun, and you won't have to explain to your mrs why her favourite vase is in bits all over the floor.

Make sure that any requests are **doable**. Your child can only do one small thing at once, so telling him to tidy his room will probably fall on deaf ears. Instead, break it down into smaller chunks, and you should get a better reaction. Or at least a reaction.

Finally, as with defiance, **prepare him** for a request well in advance, and **reward good behaviour.**

Telling Tales

"Ammm, I'm telling." These three words (if you can call the first one a word) regularly struck fear into my loins when I was a kid. It was more than likely uttered by one of my so-called 'friends', who would then run off and tell on me to a teacher/my mum/anyone who was nearby.

When your child comes up to you and tells tales, it is important that you tread carefully. If you dismiss each one, then your kid may not let you know if Timmy from next door is playing with matches underneath your car. If you punish the other kid every single time, then your child is learning that telling tales is acceptable and that he never has to fight his own battles.

I just called my kid a 'tell tale tit'. Now he's laughing. What do I do?

Don't call him that, for a start. Make sure you **assess the situation** each time your child approaches you, and decide whether or not the tale is to do with something that is dangerous or just simply annoying. If it's dangerous, then your child is right to tell you.

If you've decided that the tale has no substance, and is just your child trying to get attention or get one over on his mates, then **do not get involved.** Calmly inform him that telling tales is wrong, and that he needs to sort out the situation himself. This will help him gain independence, confidence and improve his problem-solving skills.

You could always give your child extra work so **telling tales isn't worth his while.** For example, explain that you are too busy to deal with it right now, but that your child should draw you a picture of what happened. Chances are, unless he's the next Andy Warhol, he'll get bored, give up, and go and sort it out himself: which hopefully won't include aggression, defiance, or ignoring you.

"Marilyn Monroe stole my crayons.
Here she is in all different colours."

TALKING ABOUT TRICKY SUBJECTS

Newsflash: your child will ask questions about stuff.

Scenario: You're in a crowded yet quiet supermarket with your three year-old child. You're perusing the meat aisle for a BBQ when a guy in a wheelchair coasts past. You see your child clock that a guy in a chair has just rolled by, and his eyes widen. Your buttocks clench.

Please don't, please don't, please don't…

"DADDY, WHY HAS THAT MAN GOT WHEELS FOR LEGS?!"

When you think about it, as embarrassing as this situation is, it's not that bad. Your child is just being inquisitive, and even if the disabled guy heard, he probably just thought it was funny. Nevertheless, you're now thinking of ways to climb into the meat freezer and die, surrounded by lamb cutlets and pork kebabs.

How you handle these kinds of situations, though, is very important, and goes a long way to shaping your child's perception of the world. So here's some advice on how to tackle those tricky subjects.

Disability

In your child's mind, everyone walks around fine, no-one has any long-term conditions or impairments, and Peppa Pig is the greatest thing on earth. So don't be surprised if he starts pointing at someone with only half an arm.

If your child does notice that someone has a disability, **talk to them** about the differences between people. Explain that some people can't see, or some can't walk. **Keep things simple**, as your child isn't so interested that he wants a ten minute-long answer.

Make sure you **avoid calling those without a disability 'normal'**, as it implies that disabled people are somehow abnormal. Instead, **focus on their personality**, instead of their disability. If the person with a disability is a friend, then highlight the fact that they share the same hobbies, perhaps, or the same favourite colour.

Most of all, **teach respect**. Nip teasing in the bud as soon as it happens, explaining that those kinds of sayings can hurt. **Encourage interaction** between your child and a disabled person to prove that the only difference is in perception, not reality, and that disabled people are in no way inferior to those who are not disabled.

Race

At this early stage in his life, your child has little to no concept of race. Any differences in colour he notices between his skin and that of his classmates or friends is purely that: colour.

Therefore, when the issue of colour arises, **don't shy away from it**. Explain that everyone is different, and be enthusiastic about the fact that we are all unique.

Make sure he interacts with those from different ethnicities and backgrounds, and read him stories involving other cultures so that he is aware that each person is different.

Be careful what you say, as well. If you describe others as 'black' or 'white', then don't be surprised if your child starts to mimic you. **Instead, refer to others only by their names**, regardless of ethnicity.

Instil in your child the virtues of **fairness and equality**, and explain that even though skin colour might be different from person to person, we are all the same; unless you are a racist, of course, in which case I suggest you put down this book and jump off the nearest cliff.

Death

What you believe happens after you die is for you to tell your child about; but the concept of death in general is one that most preschoolers struggle to get their head around.

Chances are, following the death of a pet or family member, your kid will ask a *lot* of questions. It is important that you **answer him directly,** giving **brief and simple answers** that he will be able to understand with his tiny preschool brain. Explain that bodies simply stop working when they're old, but that the pet/person does not feel any pain.

Beware of frightening your child with intense bereavement, but **explain that grown-ups cry** and that it is acceptable to feel sad.

Remember the deceased in a positive light. Whether a pet or a person, talk to your child about all the great times they both had. Encourage your child to draw the deceased a picture or light a candle in memory of them.

Make sure that your **child's life remains structured**. The regularity of the day – going to bed on time, going to school on time – will help reassure your child and give them a sense of safety.

MAKING ROOM FOR MUMMY AND DADDY TIME

Because it'd be nice if - just once - the kids didn't cry halfway through.

I'm really sorry if I offend you with this statement. If you're easily insulted, look away now; but I wouldn't bother, because you won't know when to look back.

Pretty much my favourite time of the day is when both my kids are in bed.

I can hear you gasping in horror. Don't get me wrong: I love spending time with my two boys, and watching them grow up and learn new things every day is an absolute joy. But they're hard work. Being a parent is hard work. And so, when they're both in bed, my wife and I can slump onto the settee, exhale deeply, and revel in the silence.

If you're really honest with yourself, you agree with me. Go on, admit it.

Being a parent is a full-time job, and as much as you love your kids, there are times when you may pine for the days when it was just you and your partner, and you could do whatever the heck you wanted. You could lie in on weekends, go out until the wee hours, or just slob around in your pyjamas all day, if you wanted to. These feelings may bring on pangs of guilt, but wanting to spend time with your spouse or partner, just the two of you, is perfectly natural.

In fact, it's healthy. Studies have shown that many couples note a significant decline in their relationship once they have children. It's not because they suddenly despise each other, but because they no longer have the time to spend alone. Therefore, making the time to spend with just you and your partner is an important part of being a parent.

Tell me how it's done.

Cut out the TV. Whilst seeing how Phil Mitchell et al are getting on in Albert Square might be one good way to spend an evening, you end up sitting on the settee not talking to each other before going to bed and falling asleep. Try having a few nights where you switch off the TV and spend some quality time together. (No, not in that way. Your mind is so dirty. Although…)

Date nights. Date nights are a recurring feature in the lives of many parents, and they are a great way of spending some time together. Enlist the help of a babysitter (or, if all else fails, your in-laws), and go out for a meal together, or to a show – whatever it is that you both love doing. Just enjoy spending time with one another without having a weeping child clinging onto your trouser leg the whole time.

Take up a hobby together. Whether it's ballroom dancing, clay pigeon shooting, or going to a book club, find a common hobby that you both enjoy and make sure you schedule some time in each week to indulge yourselves in something you can enjoy or bond over.

Go to bed at the same time. So often my wife and I will go to bed at different times. She'll head upstairs as soon as Holby City is over, and I'll spend another hour or two surfing the Internet, or writing about how you shouldn't go to bed at different times. If you both get into bed at the same time, you've got a few more moments to spend together until one of you falls asleep. And yes: Sex. I knew you'd make me say it.

"He said 'Sex'!"

TRAVELLING WITH KIDS

Are we nearly there yet?

At the time of writing, my kids are both young enough to fall asleep if you drive for a long enough period of time. But I'm well aware that, pretty soon, my car journeys will be punctuated every minute with those five little words we all dread to hear.

Short of dividing the front and back of your car with a six-inch thick piece of glass, you are inevitably going to be stuck on long journeys with a kid kicking the back of your seat and whinging at you every five minutes. Fortunately, if you're well prepared and totally deaf, driving with kids in the back can be a pretty chilled out experience.

Before You Go

There's one of those horrible business jargon sayings that goes 'fail to prepare, prepare to fail'.

"Yeeees, I made it up myself, don'tcha know.
So utterly clever."

The irksome thing is that when getting ready to go on a long journey, preparation really is the key.

Take a load of **games, puzzles and activities** to keep him occupied on the way – even a DVD player, if you don't mind your child getting carsick and vomming all over the back of your neck.

If you're going abroad, **plan your vaccinations** well in advance, and be careful not to take your child to anywhere where exotic diseases are rife, or the weather so hot/cold that you'll all end up completely miserable.

Stock up on **healthy snacks** to keep rumbling stomachs – which soon leads to full-on shrieking – at bay. **Take plenty of water** as well.

Make sure the **car space is as comfortable as possible**: your kid will freak if he's squashed between a suitcase and thirteen cushions.

If you're flying to your destination, **book seats near the exit and toilets.** This will give you (and your child) plenty of leg room as well as a short distance to walk to get to the loo, thus preventing him from clambering over four rows of seats and countless passengers just to do a wee.

As well as any prescription medication your child might be on, **stock up on painkillers** and other basic medical supplies such as plasters, as you never know when you might need them.

On the Journey

Make sure you **break up long journeys** by taking regular breaks. Not only will it give your child the chance to run around and let off steam, but it'll keep you alert as well. The last thing you want is to do all that packing just to fall asleep at the wheel and end up bonnet-first in the Thames.

Even better, **find somewhere on the way** between you and your destination to visit for a short while. This will give your child something to look forward to and hopefully keep him quiet.

Finally, **don't expect too much of your kids**. They're just as excited as you are, but don't quite have the same level of self-control.

Or rugged handsomeness, you stud.

RANDOM BITS

This is a collection of bits that don't fit into either 'Baby', 'Infant' or 'Preschool', so they're a tad random.

Many of these bits are pieces I've written for various parenting publications. I've reprinted them here in case you missed them the first time, and also to pad the book out a bit. I hope you understand.

ANNOYING THINGS OTHER PEOPLE DO WITH YOUR KIDS

I consider myself to be a rather laid-back person, y'know, pretty chilled out.

I'm not completely horizontal, though. There are certain things that bug me: crunching, for example. I detest the sound - whether it's cereal, lettuce, apples, or whatever. Since becoming a father, the list of annoyances has grown.

The same things, I've noticed, happen time and time again, and really wind me up. After talking to other parents, it seems I'm not alone: so, I've decided to share them with you, in no particular order.

People Won't Return Your Child

I have no problem with other people holding my baby, as long as I know who they are and they don't run off with him. But I'd like to think that if I was holding someone else's baby, and that baby started crying, that I would return the aforementioned infant to his or her parent.

Bizarrely, this logic is lost on some people, who insist on keeping hold of your baby even when he's screaming his head off, trying desperately to soothe him by bouncing him up and down and cooing in his face. "He doesn't want you," I scream in my head, "he wants me! Give him back!" And then I spend the next 10 minutes resisting the urge to rugby tackle the offender to the ground and wrestle my baby from his/her arms.

Making Your Kid Laugh During Discipline

We're trying out the naughty step system of discipline with our three-year-old at the moment, with limited success. The first time I tried it, he laughed hysterically for the full three minutes and was largely unrepentant. Since then, though, he's twigged that when he's on the naughty step he needs to sit quietly and contemplate his misdemeanours.

Which is why it really doesn't help when someone else – usually a doting family member – comes along and starts messing around with him when he's on the step, when he should be utterly remorseful. In one fell swoop, your discipline has gone out the window and you're left seething as your kid forgets all about why the naughty thing he did was naughty in the first place.

Rubbing Perfume on Your Baby's Face

We've all got them; the elderly female relative who gives your baby a bear-hug, trapping him in her cavernous cleavage while she shrieks about how gorgeous he is. This is fine: nothing wrong with showing a bit of love and affection.

What I do object to, though, is having a baby handed back to me that has been rubbed so much against a liver-spotted chest and neck that it reeks of Eau de Arthritis and the faint whiff of wee. It literally takes days of washing and three bottles of Febreze to get that smell out.

Allowing Their Kid to Crawl All Over You

I don't have a phobia of other kids or anything. But as you watch on and snigger as your snotty-nosed, sticky-fingered little brat toddles up to me and crawls all over my lap, I think I'm entitled to wrinkle my nose and make little kicking motions to try and dissuade it from slobbering all over my thigh. I don't let my kid vomit all over your jeans, and would appreciate it if you did the same.

The same thing applies to parents who insist that their toddler kisses everyone in the room goodbye. You're sat there, awaiting your turn with trepidation. How do I kiss her? A peck on the cheek that shows I don't really want to be here? Or a full-blown snog that could land me in jail?

In the end, you go for the cheek-kiss. But not before the little angel has wiped a smear of snot all over your chin.

Talking to You Through Your Kid

Parents and in-laws are the worst for this one. When you decide that you're not going to take your baby out for a walk, or swimming, for example, they tell you off. But instead of having to go through the awkward rigmarole of doing it to your face, they do it through your child. "Isn't daddy a big meanie?" they say, or: "Daddy only wants to watch TV, doesn't he?"

Well, yes, I do want to watch TV. But that's only because I need some rest after being up in the night with him for three hours. So stuff you, judgemental expletive.

FIVE WAYS IN WHICH BEING A DAD CHANGES YOU

People always told me that having kids changes you, that it turns you into a completely different person. I always reacted in the same way I did when they told me that having kids was hard: with a disbelieving look, perhaps a 'pfff' of incredulity, and a certain smugness that I wouldn't be fazed by becoming a parent whatsoever.

Well, they were right about the kids being hard bit, and they're right about kids changing you.

Now, I've never been a particularly masculine person; I'm certainly no alpha male. I regularly lose to my three year-old son in arm wrestling competitions, and people snigger at me when I struggle to lift weights at the gym. But I was never a particularly emotional person: I always took things in my stride, and never cried. That rhymed. Unintentional.

Now I'm a seasoned pro at being a father, I can see a distinct difference in myself now to the carefree singleton I once was. The weediness remains, unfortunately, but there are five main things that have changed since I've become a dad:

I'm super sensitive

Whereas before you could have showed me the most heart-breaking and tear-jerking films known to man and I would remain stony-faced, now even the slightest thing brings a tear to my eye. I get all quivery-lipped when antelopes get eaten by cheetahs on wildlife programmes. I blink back stinging tears when I read heart-warming news stories about long-lost friends who have been reunited after decades apart. The other day I watched a documentary about pregnancy and almost had to leave the room. What's happened to me? I never used to cry, and now I don't dare watch 'Love Actually' in case I spend the entire time blubbing into the bosom of my confused (and very embarrassed) wife.

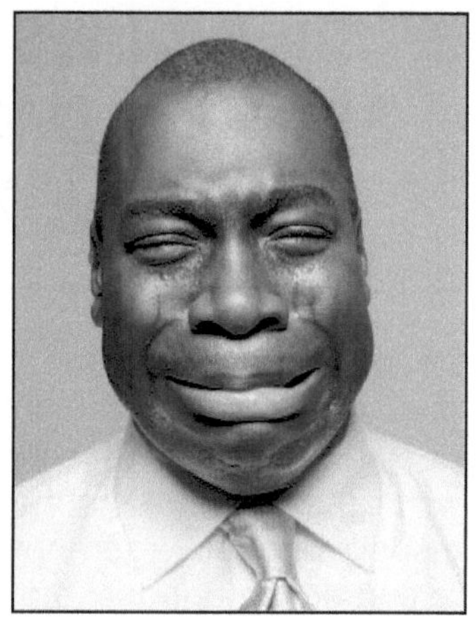

I'm immune to poo

I remember once, when I was childless and fresh-faced, walking my in-laws' dog; and as dogs are wont to do, it left a nice little deposit for me on a grass verge. Being a considerate kind of fellow, and armed with a handy little black bag, I reluctantly set about picking up the aforementioned turd using the bag as a glove and throwing it into the nearest bin.

It literally took me ten minutes and endless bouts of dry retching before I could even bring myself to touch the poo. For hours afterwards I felt dirty. Now, my eight month-old son could projectile poo all over me, and I wouldn't bat an eyelid. I wouldn't be happy about it, sure, but I certainly wouldn't freak out like I used to.

I eat food incredibly fast

Gone are the days when I could savour every mouthful of my medium-rare steak, washing it down with a sip of red wine. Now, when time is of the essence and as rare as gold dust, with over-tired children shrieking in my ears, I gobble down my food with all the grace and dignity of a pack of wolves during feeding time at the zoo. Sometimes, I don't even have time to use my hands. I've been banned from almost every restaurant in my home town for this very behaviour.

I'm super-protective

I'm not going to be vying for the title of World's Strongest Man any time soon, but you even suggest that you're going to upset either one of my children and I'll start bursting out of my shirt like the Incredible Hulk and develop some kind of super-strength.

I know for a fact every parent can relate to this point; the mere thought of your child being saddened by something makes your blood boil and your eyes pop. So be warned: I may look stringy and feeble, but I'm not afraid to scratch if it means defending my family.

I'm clued up on pregnancy terms

I've completely embraced my feminine side. I could sit and talk to an expectant mother for hours about her softened cervix, mucous levels and tender breasts, whether she was happy to do so or not. I can tell you all about the fonatelle, Couvade Syndrome and your perineum. What do you mean, do I want to talk about the football? Forget that! How's your colostrum production lately?

THINGS I WISH I KNEW BEFORE I HAD KIDS

You know as well as I do that friends and family just love to dish out advice, especially in the final days of pregnancy. Except that it's not really advice. "You're not going to get any sleep now" isn't advice. Neither is "Breastfeeding can be really painful". Sucking in through pursed lips, shaking your head and smugly stating "I'm glad I'm not you" is definitely not advice.

There are some things that I wish someone had told me before I had kids: ideally, before the thought of a kid was but a mere twinkle in my eye. Just little snippets of information that I can actually use when I become a parent, that's all I'm after. So, here's what I wish someone had told me before I had children.

Lie-ins will not be a part of weekends for at least ten years

Now, I'm not stupid; I know that with a baby comes a considerable reduction in uninterrupted sleep. I knew before I became a dad that the days of crawling out of a sweaty bed at midday on Saturday would be a thing of the past. But I assumed I'd still get to sleep until 8, maybe even 9 in the morning. Nope: I now class half six as a lie-in. If I'm really lucky, I might get to 7am, but it rarely happens. Thanks a lot, children.

Babies don't just poo...they poo a LOT

I read a statistic somewhere once which said that newborns go through about ten nappies a day.

That's about 300 a month. Nearly 4,000 per year. I guess I just assumed I'd be wiping poo off my baby's buttocks two, three times a day maximum. But it's almost relentless; nothing fills you with despair more than the squelch of another deposit being made at the nappy bank, although the faces they pull can be pretty funny.

I'd need to take out a second mortgage

I've always been aware that bringing up a child is expensive, but I wouldn't have expected to go without clothes just so I can have the money to buy yet another multipack of nappies. Formula milk is just as expensive: unfortunately, despite our best efforts, breastfeeding was just too painful for my wife when feeding my second little boy, and so he's been chugging on Cow & Gate for the last few months. It's over £8 a tub! Can't I just feed him Sainsbury's Basics apple juice?!

I'd get excited about trains and tractors

Suddenly, and quite inexplicably, my childhood fascination with large vehicles has returned after having children. I find myself pointing at tractors even when there's no-one else in the car. I'm dreading the time I'm driving my boss somewhere and halfway through the journey I exclaim "Oooh, look! A *caravan*!"

Going out means staying in

I can't remember my last trip to the cinema. Nowadays, if we want to see a film, we wait for half a year for it to come out on DVD so we can rent it. 'Going out for a meal' really means ordering in a takeaway pizza. It's been so long since I went out at night that I've forgotten how to dance. At least, that's what I'm blaming my clunky moves on.

I'd turn into my dad

Out of all the nuggets of advice that someone could have given me, this would have been the most important. It'd mean that I could watch out for those tell-tale signs and nip them in the bud. But no-one told me that I'd end up turning into my father, and so now I find myself making the same terrible jokes as him, standing like him…I'm even nurturing the beginnings of a beer belly.

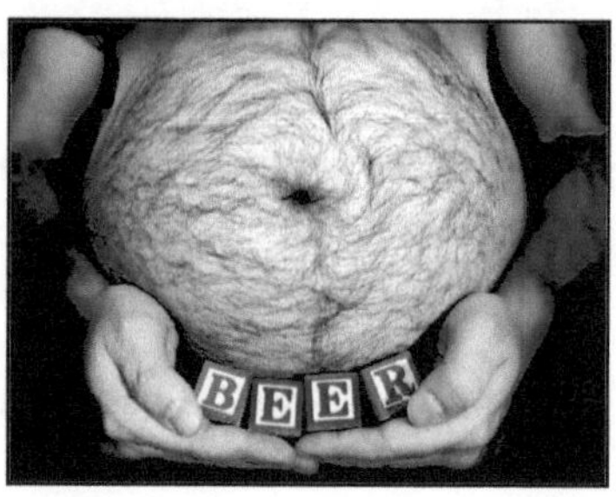

What's the moral of this story? If you've got the bright idea of dishing out advice to an expectant couple, at least make it good advice; or, a few weeks later, you might find yourself at the sharp end of a very cranky and very overtired father.

WHEN AM I GOING TO HAVE SEX AGAIN?

The question on every man's mind, dad or not

Us men are a shallow lot. No sooner has our partner gone through the pain of childbirth (which we will nev er match, I admit, even when comparing the agony to a kick in the crotch) and provided us with a beautiful child, we're thinking about doing the nasty again.

They say men think about sex once every six seconds. As a man myself, I can categorically state that this is not true: if it was, we simply wouldn't get anything done. I mean, less than we do already. But it is lingering in our mind as the day goes on, every now and then popping up to give us something to think about. What can I say? It must stem from our cavemen days.

So it's no wonder that it doesn't take long for us to wonder when we're going to have sex again after childbirth: which is why you might find us every now and then looking like we're about to ask you a question, having a second thought, and then carrying on watching the TV without saying a word. We're not stupid, despite what you may think: us dads know that for a few weeks after childbirth, our partner is not feeling at her very best. We sympathise, and know that you must be incredibly sore 'down there', which explains why you're walking like John Wayne. But it'd be great to know how you feel, what you're thinking when it comes to the 'S' word. And so, using the power of the Internet, I asked a group of mums for their stories.

Understandably, very few of them wanted to be named. But their stories shed a little light on the answer to the question that has plagued men since the beginning of time; and some responses were quite surprising. Instead of shying away from sex for months after birth, some mums couldn't wait to get back in the sack – depending on the severity of any damage done during labour, of course.

"I delivered my son naturally, no grazing, no tears, stitches, etc.," said one mum, "and nine days after delivery we did it for the first time…we took it very slowly." Some mothers waited marginally longer. "I was ready to try again when Lizzie was about two weeks old, but was worried that everything hadn't quite returned to normal – so we waited until six weeks." How was it, may I ask? "OMG! It was like my first time all over again!"

You stallion, you.

Some mothers understandably do not feel at their sexiest following birth. "My sex drive returned after about four months," mentioned one mum. "That doesn't mean I am up for it though; I still feel fat and wobbly and don't want him to see me naked just yet! Plus, being so tired and so devoted to a new baby means even if you do fancy it, you rarely have the energy or time."

Good point. Being up at all hours of the night doesn't do much for your stamina levels, and as a result time to bond between the sheets can be few and far between. This can get frustrating for both mum and dad, who are keen to have a bit of 'alone time' despite the shriek of constant crying perforating the air.

So, were the dads pushing for sex? Far from it, if you look at the mums' stories. In fact, we find that us dads are a caring bunch. "One week later I was desperate to get back in the saddle, despite the pain and discomfort," one mum recalls. "but it was the other half who wasn't sure! Normal service resumed at two weeks." "I wanted to try after two weeks," said another mum, "but my other half said no."

"My other half ensured me that if it was too uncomfortable he would stop." remembers a mum. "He was gentle, and what made things so much easier was that he was so understanding about it. My advice would be to relax, take it slowly; and a bit point for the males is to give us support and understanding!"

So there you have it. Although us dads are thinking about sex, it turns out that we've come a long way since the days we lived in caves and grunted at each other. Plus, we're mindful that your hormones are raging, which is why we look so scared all the time.

What He's Thinking

"I want to have sex again but she might claw my face off if I mention it."

"I hope I don't hurt her, that'd really ruin the mood."

"I can hear the baby moving in the other room. Please, please don't wake up…"

What She's Thinking

"Damn, I'm sore. Do you think people have noticed that I'm walking funny?"

"I want to have sex again but am worried it might hurt."

"Urgh, look at me. When am I going to shift this baby weight?"

"I can hear the baby moving in the other room. Please, please don't wake up…"

Top Things Dads Should Never Say

"You feel a bit bigger."

"These stretch marks...are they going to go eventually?"

"I miss when you had big boobs."

"We should've asked them to stitch you up tighter."

"Are you going on a diet any time soon?"

THE DIFFERENCE BETWEEN DADS AND NON-DADS

Two men meet in a hotel restaurant one morning for breakfast. One is called Barry, the other Dave. It's the morning after their office party, where both men had drunk incredible amounts of alcohol and retired to their respective rooms with their wives. Dave turns to Barry.

"Last night, did you…y'know?"

Barry grins. "Yep. All night."

"All night? Wow!"

"The mrs said it was really deep." Barry stirs coffee, still grinning.

"It certainly was a night to remember," says the other, beaming.

Barry looks out of the window, pondering. "It's been a long time since I've been able to go that long."

"Really?" inquires Dave. "Must have been the alcohol."

"And the lack of crying kids."

Dave's brow furrows in confusion. "The lack of crying kids?"

"Yep. We were asleep before our heads hit the pillow, and didn't wake up until nine this morning." Barry smiles at the pleasant memory.

Dave stares at Barry. "What are you on about?"

Barry looks at Dave. “Sleep. I’m a dad, Dave. I haven’t slept properly in three years. Why, what did you think we were talking about?”

Pause.

“Sex, Barry. Sex.”

QUOTATIONS ABOUT PARENTING

You can learn many things from children. How much patience you have, for instance.
Franklin P. Jones

Children seldom misquote. In fact, they usually repeat word for word what you shouldn't have said.
Author Unknown

A child is a curly dimpled lunatic.
Ralph Waldo Emerson

Do your kids a favor - don't have any.
Robert Orben

Anyone who thinks the art of conversation is dead ought to tell a child to go to bed.
Robert Gallagher

It is easier to build strong children than to repair broken men.
Frederick Douglass

FINAL THOUGHTS

Like Jerry Springer, but without the fighting midgets.

It's funny, really: at the end of each day, when your kid is in bed, you flake out on the sofa, beer in hand, and think about how darn stressful being a dad is.

But look back over the time you've been a dad, and try and remember the constant stress. You can't. It's as if your brain has blocked out the memories, and instead all you remember is the great time you've had being a father. Playing on the swings, carrying him on your shoulders, those midnight kisses when he's crying for a feed. They say time flies when you're having fun, and I can remember the day my eldest was born as if it were yesterday.

Being a dad isn't all rough and tumble fun and games, though. It's our job to set an example for our kids, because – believe it or not – they see you as a role model, an example...maybe even a hero.

Sure, you'll make a few mistakes along the way, we all do. No-one's perfect, and if they say they are, they're lying, which instantly makes them not perfect. But being a dad is a steep learning curve: it's not something that can be taught, it's something you teach yourself. Learn lessons when things go wrong, and don't be afraid to pat yourself on the back when you do something right.

Not only is being a dad the source of great responsibility and a dollop of pressure, but it's also one of the most terrifying things you can do. You spend every minute of every day petrified that something bad is going to happen: that they're going to fall ill, or have a nasty accident; they're going to mix with the wrong crowd at school, or that you're going to set a terrible example and screw up your kid beyond all help.

Unfortunately, there's nothing I can say that can make you feel any better, but I don't have to. Firstly, it's not my place, and secondly, it's all part of being a dad. If anything, it's a good thing: it shows that you care about being a father.

There's no doubting that having a kid is hard work. But it's also one of the most rewarding things that can ever happen in your life. All of your previous achievements, your proudest moments – that great promotion, the awesome overhead kick you scored – pale into insignificance when your child takes his first steps, or says your name for the first time. Your little guy or girl becomes the centre of your world.

Of course, you know this already. I'm preaching to the converted. But humour me, while I prove it to you. Think hard about having a stressful day at work, or something else that's happened to you that sucks particularly badly. Feel rubbish, don't you? Sorry.

Now think about your son or daughter: their laugh, the way they walk, the funny things they say, how great it feels when they give you a hug, or how they run to meet you when you get home.

Now turn over the page.

Smiled, didn't you?

Knew you would.

www.ingramcontent.com/pod-product-compliance
Ingram Content Group UK Ltd.
Pitfield, Milton Keynes, MK11 3LW, UK
UKHW040602210726
13854UKWH00008B/1834

9 781447 530930